EXPLORING APPRENTICESHIP CAREERS

$5.97 10-80

EXPLORING APPRENTICESHIP CAREERS

By
Charlotte Lobb

RICHARDS ROSEN PRESS, INC.
New York, N.Y. 10010

Published in 1978 by Richards Rosen Press, Inc.
29 East 21st Street, New York, N.Y. 10010

First Edition

Library of Congress Cataloging in Publication Data

Lobb, Charlotte.
Exploring apprenticeship careers.

1. Apprentices—United States. 2. Vocational guidance—United States. I. Title.
HD4885.U5L55 331.5′5′023 77–22688
ISBN 0–8239–0403–2

Manufactured in the United States of America

To
CHUCK
With Thanks

About the Author

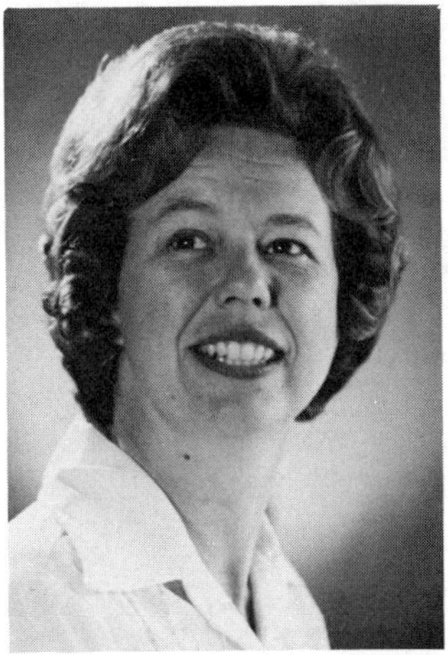

Charlotte Lobb, a native Californian, graduated from the University of Southern California (1956, cum laude) with a Bachelor of Science degree in Personnel and Industrial Relations. For five years she was employed in the aerospace industry, screening, interviewing, and placing applicants in jobs ranging from "coffee girl" to "lab analyst."

Involved in her community, Mrs. Lobb is Chairperson of the City of Torrance Manpower Council, the citizen advisory group for the administration of federally funded employment programs, and a member of the Board of Directors of the South Bay–Harbor Voluntary Action Center; she is also active in the Torrance League of Women Voters.

As a teacher in the Torrance Adult School, Mrs. Lobb conducts classes in job-hunting techniques and making career decisions.

In addition to the career-guidance books *Exploring Careers Through Volunteerism* (1976) and *Exploring Careers Through Part-Time and Summer Employment* (1977), Mrs. Lobb has both fiction and nonfiction magazine articles to her credit and writes two regular newspaper columns.

Her husband, Charles Lobb, is an engineering manager with Hughes Aircraft Company. They have two daughters, Carolyn and Patricia.

Photos by the author.

Preface

While researching this book, I reached several conclusions:

It is harder to become an apprentice than it is to go to college.

There is no room for high-school dropouts in the apprentice business—the competition is too great.

Today's apprentices are among this country's most conscientious, committed, and hard-working young people. They are each truly proud of the craft they are learning.

Apprentices are super people!

This book is written for the young person who gets through math and science classes in high school but who finds the shop classes—auto repair, woodworking, metal shop—the kind of challenge he or she prefers.

It is for the person who likes to make something with his or her hands and then stand back with pride to say, "I did that."

This book is for those people who feel that apprenticeship training as an alternate form of post-high-school learning is neither better nor worse than college—it just happens to be right for them.

Through this book I hope to help these people get from wherever they are now—in junior high, high school or as recent graduates—into an apprenticeship program.

To do this, I interviewed real, live apprentices as well as their bosses, their teachers, employment interviewers, and field coordinators of apprenticeship programs. The reader will have a chance to meet these people and get to know them. The reader will learn how the apprentices got their jobs, what is interesting and what is dull about the work, what the boss looks for when interviewing applicants, and how the apprentice views himself. The reader should gain an understanding of what it is like to be an apprentice.

Additionally, basic facts about the crafts are provided, plus brief descriptions of trade-school classes normally taken by apprentices.

There are more than 300 apprenticeable trades in the United States. Below is a list of the most common trades which involve such broad information that they usually require apprenticeship rather than simply on-the-job training. (The number of years of apprenticeship required is in parentheses.) Not all of these occupations or training programs for them are available in all areas of the country.

Aircraft Fabricator (3–4)
Airplane Mechanic (3–4)
Arborist (3)
Asbestos Worker (4)
Automobile Body Repairman (4)
Automobile Mechanic (4)
Baker (3)
Barber (2)
Blacksmith (4)
Boilermaker (4)
Bookbinder (4–5)
Brewer (2)
Bricklayer (3–4)
Butcher, Meatcutter (3)
Cabinetmaker (4)
Candy Maker (3–4)
Canvas Worker (3)
Carman (4)
Carpenter (4)
Cement Mason (3)
Chef (3)
Cosmetician (2)
Dental Technician (3–4)
Designer (5)
Draftsman (4)
Electrician (4–5)
Electroplater (3)
Electrotyper (6)
Embalmer (2)
Engraver (5)
Fabric Cutter (3–4)
Farm Equipment Mechanic (3–4)
Floor Coverer (3–4)
Foundryman (2–4)

Furrier (3–4)
Glazier–Glass Worker (2–4)
Heat Treater (4)
Iron Worker (2–4)
Jeweler (2–3)
Land Surveyor (5)
Lather (3–4)
Lead Burner (5)
Leather Worker (3–4)
Lithographer (4–5)
Machinist (4)
Mailer (4–5)
Metal Polisher and Buffer (3)
Millwright (4)
Model Maker (4)
Musical Instrument Mechanic (3–4)
Office Machine Repairer (3)
Operating Engineer (3–4)
Optical Technician (4)
Orthopedic Technician (3–4)
Painter and Decorator (2–3)
Patternmaker (5)
Photoengraver (5–6)
Photographer, Commercial (3)
Plasterer (3–4)
Plate Printer (4)
Plumber–Pipe Fitter (4–5)
Printer (4)
Printing Pressman (4)
Refrigeration and Air Conditioning Mechanic (5)
Rigger (2–4)
Roofer (2–3)
Rotogravure Engraver (5–6)
Sheet Metal Worker (3–4)
Sign and Pictorial Painter (3–4)
Silversmith (3–4)
Stationary Engineer (4)
Stereotyper (5–6)
Stone Worker (2–4)
Stonemason (3)
Tailor (4)
Telephone Worker, Lineman (4)
Terrazzo Worker (3)
Textile Technician (2–4)
Tile Setter (3)
Tool and Diemaker (4–5)
Upholsterer (3–4)
Wallpaper Craftsman (4–5)
Wire Weaver (3–4)

Only a limited number of trades can be discussed in a book of this size, so I have made an effort to select a variety of skills. The reader can assume that what is said about one trade—carpentry, for instance—will be generally true for a related trade, such as painting, although the latter is not discussed at length.

Much of the statistical information in the book was taken

from *Occupational Outlook Handbook 1976–77*. I suggest that readers check the most recent editions of that book for current information on wages and job prospects.

Other chapters discuss women in apprentice careers, military training as an alternative, and the importance of high-school courses.

I would like to thank all of those people who took the time and trouble to share their knowledge with me. I hope that through their words, now shared with the readers, young people will be encouraged to follow in their footsteps to a satisfying job and career in the skilled trades.

Charlotte Lobb

Contents

EXPLORING APPRENTICESHIP CAREERS

Chapter I

Routes to Apprenticeship Training

Apprenticeship is the centuries-old way of learning a skilled trade. Throughout recorded history, a master craftsman —a goldsmith, a blacksmith, a cart builder, a printer—would employ indentured apprentices. These youngsters, sometimes as young as ten or twelve, would live with the master or journeyman and learn the trade step by step under close supervision. Eventually, the apprentice would himself be considered a master and might open his own business.

Nowadays, apprenticeship doesn't begin until age eighteen, and the apprentice doesn't move in with the master. But apprenticeship training still provides a recognized method of becoming thoroughly skilled in many trades.

The route a young person must take to become an apprentice depends primarily on how unionized his desired trade is in his geographic area. A closed-shop union in which all apprentice applicants are tested and rank-order listed for admission to the program requires a different route than landing a nonunion job with a small independent shop.

Here are the routes young people have successfully taken to become an apprentice:

1. Connections
2. Testing

3. School
4. Tenacity
5. Starting at a lower job

Connections

Having connections, an uncle or a father in the trade, has been the age-old way to land a job as an apprentice. In some trades in this country a solid connection was absolutely the only way to gain entry into the industry, and for many other trades the connection was valuable.

Connections are still important in trades that do not have a closed union shop or hiring hall arrangement, or where the industry is made up of many small, owner-operated shops. Connections can also be helpful in avoiding periods of unemployment in the construction industry.

Here are some ways connections can work.

Jerry Collins landed his job as an apprentice printer because his sister was working in the bindery department of a middle-sized printing firm. The employer has a steady stream of young applicants, many equally qualified for an entry-level job, so he relies on personal recommendations of friends, current employees, and associates in the trade.

Pete Hindman started work in his father's small upholstery shop when he was fourteen. He worked summers and weekends until he graduated from high school. Pete learned his trade both from his father and from related trade-school classes. Now he is the owner-operator of the shop, and his teenage son is helping with the business.

Evan Jouliane was accepted as an apprentice carpenter because his father's friend, a contractor, guaranteed to the union that there was employment available for Evan. The employer has a special interest in Evan's future and has made an effort not to lay him off during slow periods. And Evan works hard on the job to justify the boss's faith in him.

Young people are often disheartened when they feel they don't have a connection that will lead them to satisfactory employment. In reality, there are people all around who may prove to be excellent connections.

If your relatives are not in any trade that interests you, how about your neighbors? Do you even know what kind of jobs they hold? Your mother probably knows, or you can ask.

Maybe your dad has an old high-school friend who is a plumber or floor coverer. If you are interested in the trade, ask your father to talk with his friend.

School teachers, Scout leaders, ministers, and your own friends hear about job openings and may become that connection you are seeking.

It is important to let as many people as possible know that you are looking for work. A connection may not pay off right away. It may be six months or a year later when you get a call, "Hey, buddy, you still looking for a job? I know a place that is hiring."

Testing

Formalized testing of apprentice applicants is most common in the construction trades. Major contractors are permitted to hire only union members. It is a joint committee of union and management representatives, not the employer, that decides who may enter an apprentice program. Once on the job, however, an employee who does not work up to the employer's standards can be fired or laid off.

Electrician and plumber unions in the Los Angeles area accept new applications for only a short period once each year, and occasionally, when construction is slow, even less often. (Some unions may accept applications all year and notify applicants of the date of examinations.)

The secret, then, for someone interested in the trade is to determine when the union will be accepting applications.

How do you find out?

Dave Gee was told about the application time by a journeyman operating engineer on the construction site where they were working. Dave was a laborer at the time.

State employment offices receive notification of open dates when apprentice applicants may apply.

Or you may call the union directly.

Check the yellow pages of your telephone book under "Labor Organizations." The numbers listed will probably be local hiring halls. Call one and say, "I would like to find out about becoming an apprentice." This office will probably give you the phone number of the Joint Apprenticeship Committee, the organization that supervises selection procedures. Call that number and repeat your request. They will be able to tell you when applications will again be accepted, and where.

If you have trouble finding the appropriate union listing, you may wish to contact your state's Division of Apprenticeship Standards. If there is a local office, it will be listed in the white pages of the phone book with other state offices. If there is no local office, you may write to the Division of Apprenticeship Standards, State Capitol.

Once you reach the right union or apprenticeship committee, you will be asked to complete an application.

The application forms will not differ significantly from other job application forms. You will be requested to supply information including your name, address, date of birth, social security number, arrest record, physical handicaps, and work history. Take along a list of names and addresses of former employers so that your application will be complete.

After filing your application with the union office, you will be notified of the time and place to take the examination.

The tests are standardized forms much like some you have taken in school. They are an attempt to predict the applicant's chance of success on the job in an objective way.

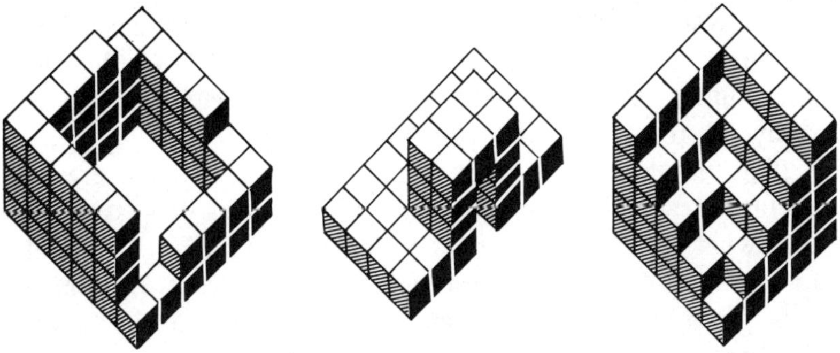

BLOCK COUNTING – COUNT THE NUMBER OF BLOCKS

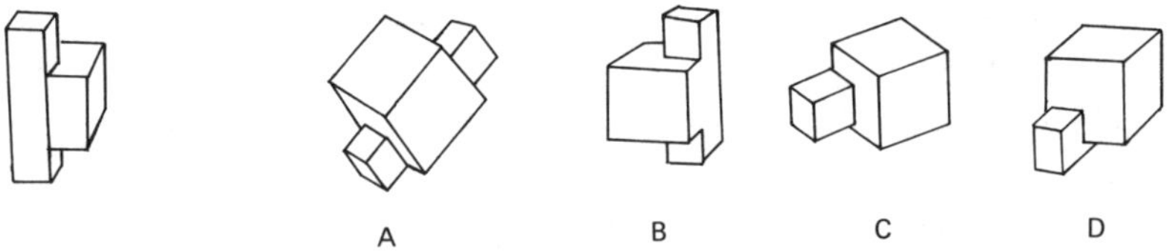

SOLID FIGURE TURNING – WHICH SHAPE, A, B, C, OR D MATCHES THE FIRST SHAPE?

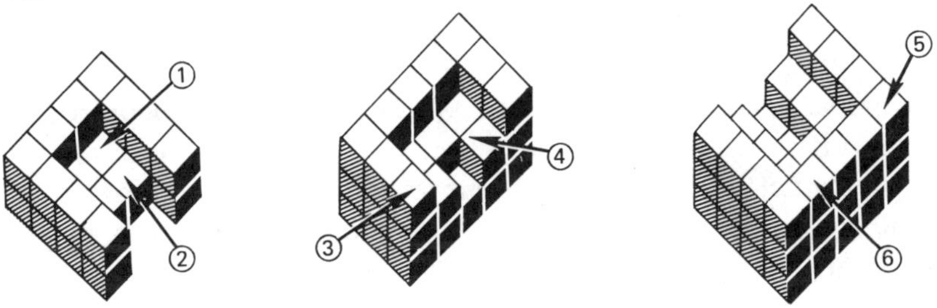

TOUCHING CUBES – HOW MANY CUBES DO THE NUMBERED CUBES TOUCH?

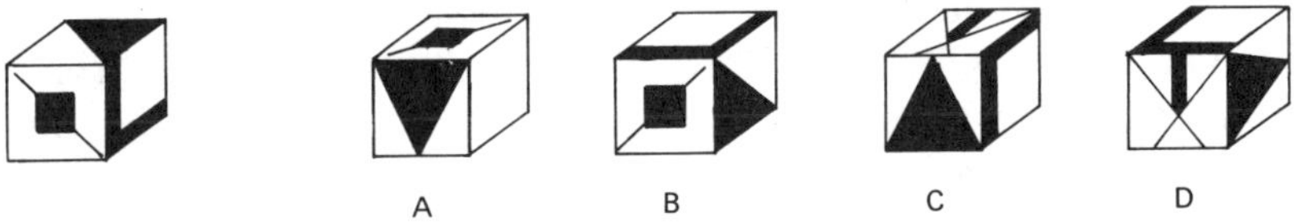

CUBE TURNING – WHICH CUBE, A, B, C, OR D MATCHES THE FIRST CUBE?

SPATIAL RELATIONS TESTS

For young people interested in giving themselves an edge in the very competitive apprentice exams, the ARCO Civil Service Test Tutor, "Apprentice, Mechanical Trades," can be a valuable study aid. It is available at your local library.

This soft-cover booklet is designed for persons who are preparing to take civil service exams. Union-sponsored tests differ somewhat from government requirements. A union is unlikely, for instance, to ask the questions on current events, history, or U.S. government that are described in the booklet. Although the booklet describes test questions on tool knowledge, many unions have dropped that portion of their tests.

Apprentice applicants should emphasize the study of sections dealing with vocabulary and reading comprehension. Most union tests include these areas.

You should also practice the exercises for mechanical insight (the ability to visualize the operation of a machine in motion, such as gears and pulleys); similarities and differences between objects; numerical problems, including fractions (brush up on algebra if you're after an electrician's job); and reading of blueprints and diagrams.

The spatial relations sections described in the booklet are also important, and similar questions will appear on almost all apprentice tests. These sections include block counting, solid figure turning, touching cubes, and cube turning. Some apprentice tests may also include questions related to visualizing figures, view, and matching parts and figures.

In addition to written tests, apprentice applicants may be asked to take manual dexterity tests. These typically involve putting pegs in the holes on a large board as fast as possible. They'll test right hand, left hand, and both hands together. There is really no way to study for this type of test, but you can hope you won't have a broken thumb on the day you have to take the test.

Some unions require an oral interview of those applicants who pass the screening test.

You will be given a time and place to appear for the interview.

The panel of interviewers will ask questions to determine how sincerely interested you are in the trade and what knowledge you have about the business. They will take note of any special health problems you may have or lack of physical strength. Your appearance will be important. And, yes, they will probably rate you higher if your dad is in the trade.

You may want to practive being interviewed, using a member of your family as the questioner. Or you can even practice alone in front of your mirror.

Make your answers concise and to the point. The interview will last fifteen to thirty minutes.

After all the applicants have taken the test and been interviewed, the top scorers will be rank-order listed.

It used to be that if there were twenty-five openings, the twenty-five top-scoring applicants would be accepted. This procedure has been modified somewhat because of affirmative action programs (the effort to provide better employment opportunities for women and minority racial groups).

The selection committee is required to look at its list of applicants to see that it meets the quota requirements for women and minority racial groups as determined by state and federal officials.

If the union is required to start five blacks in this class of apprentices and only four qualified on the initial list, the next highest black applicant will be accepted, and number twenty-five on the original list will be dropped.

Both because of affirmative action programs and the objective nature of the tests, there has never been a better time for minority persons to enter these apprentice programs. Minority classifications include Black, American Indian, Spanish Surname, Other Nonwhite, and Women.

If you qualify as a member of a minority group, it is important that you indicate this on your application. You qualify, for instance, if you are as little as 1/16th American Indian. Classifying yourself as a minority-group member, where appropriate, gives you two chances to land the job. Either you score so high on the test that you qualify as one of the top candidates, or you are rated lower on the list but are needed to meet quota requirements. Anglo males have to score very well in order to land the job.

If you feel you would be happy in a career in any one of the major construction trades—electrician, plumber, operating engineer—then by all means begin the application process with each of the appropriate unions. Even in the best of circumstances, it may take two years to begin as an apprentice. By filing several applications your odds for early employment should increase.

School

Craig Perry was working at a gas station during the day and attending auto mechanic night classes at a community college. When he told the instructor he was looking for a better job, the instructor, a daytime garage owner, hired him.

Lillian Scrogs was referred to her job as an appliance repairman based on the referral of her instructor at the local occupational center.

Glenn Sarpy's high-school print shop teacher knew of an opening in the trade and suggested that he apply.

Teachers at all levels of education become known in the trade. Employers get used to calling them for good students interested in real career opportunities. Night-class teachers who work days in the trade seem to be among the very best connections a young person can have.

Some trade schools have a formal placement service for both their current students and recent graduates. They won't guarantee you a job, but they will assist you in your job search. And employers do use this service, which amounts to a free employment agency.

If you are having trouble landing that first job, enroll in related classes, either day or evening. Do well in those classes. You will be gaining practical information that will later help you on the job, and you will be building your first contacts in the trade.

Federally funded training programs may also be available to help some persons.

The Comprehensive Employment and Training Act (CETA) provides federal money to train disadvantaged and underemployed workers.

Fidel Ramirez attended a CETA pre-employment program for carpenters. Barry Woodard did the same thing for tool and diemakers. They were paid $50 per week to attend the school. Following graduation, they were quickly placed on jobs and now have a solid employment future.

Your state employment office will know of any available CETA programs in your area.

Tenacity

Bill Majors applied at the same plumbing shop six times in eighteen months before he was hired.

"I think the boss just got tired of my coming around so often so he hired me," says Bill.

Small shops in trades such as plumbing, floor covering, and upholstery seldom have openings for new apprentices, and they have a fairly large number of applicants. In order to get the job, you may really have to impress the boss with your sincerity and interest. And you have to be there at the right time—the day after someone quits, for instance.

Reapplying at the same shops once every two or three months is acceptable and one way to succeed.

Another young plumber-to-be was so anxious to get the job that he volunteered to work two weeks without pay. Such an arrangement is illegal in terms of wage and hour laws, but it worked for this fellow. It was his way of saying he was completely committed to a career in plumbing.

Starting at a Lower Job

Meat cutter apprentices like Shawn Tanaka are almost always selected from the ranks of interested box boys and clerks already employed by the grocery store chain.

It is not uncommon in office machine repair to start as a helper–errand runner. After the boss is sure that the young person is reliable and responsible, he will encourage training both on and off the job.

Many machinists learn their trade by starting as a lathe operator in a job shop. They do one task until they can do it in their sleep. They are laid off when the job is over. And the next job shop offers an opportunity to learn a different task or another machine.

Taking a job in the industry even if it is not quite the job you would like is like school: it gives you a start, a chance to prove yourself. It gives you your first contacts in the industry. It's a beginning, and everyone has to begin somewhere.

It takes the average apprentice about two years to land the job he wants. The delay may be because of the infrequent testing procedures, the number of places where applications must be made, or the fact that many employers prefer to hire apprentices who are twenty to twenty-three years old. The average age of apprentices attending the related night school classes appears to be going up.

So what are you going to do in the meantime?

Military training (discussed in Chapter XXI) is certainly one option. It is a way to gain skills, become more employable, and grow older at the same time.

If you choose to remain a civilian, try for a job in or close to the industry in which your chosen trade is practiced.

If you work as a salesman in a hardware store, for instance, you will meet contractors who may later be willing to hire you. Lumberyard sales would provide the same sort of possible connections.

If you want to be a chef, start somewhere, anywhere, as a bus boy.

Your route to an apprentice job may be any one of the five listed. Young people have successfully traveled them all, but you won't know which one will work for you until you try. Fortunately, you can start down all the roads at once.

Tell your friends about your career goals so they can help. File applications with the appropriate unions and take their exams. Attend a trade school either day or night. Find a job that will help you toward your goal. Keep at it. It is not easy to become an apprentice, and only the very best, most committed young people succeed.

Chapter **II**

High School Courses

How often has your English teacher handed you back a paper with an "F" on it because she couldn't read your handwriting?

If you are applying for a job at a plumbing shop, the boss will hand you back your application with "No, thanks" if he can't read it.

A surprising number of jobs require the basic tool of legible handwriting. The boss knows that if a customer gets an estimate or a bill for $200 on a repair job and can't read it, the customer is unhappy. So he just doesn't hire anyone with poor handwriting. (Reasonable spelling will be a factor, too.)

Your same English teacher knows that in the 20th century no one can get by without adequate reading skills. An auto mechanic has to be able to read the repair manual. A chef has to be able to read and understand recipes. A carpenter has to be able to read a road map well enough to find the construction site that is 20 miles from home—he can't memorize that many corners and turns.

Your teachers have been telling you all through school to learn the subject so that you'll be ready for the next grade level.

What your teachers should be saying, and what you need to understand, is that each subject is preparing you for survival. The more knowledge you can master, the better you will survive.

Some courses taught at the high-school level are particularly important to students interested in a career in a skilled trade.

Basic math is absolutely essential in most apprenticeable trades. The carpenter needs to add, subtract, and understand measurements. The printer works with fractions of an inch when he must cut paper or leave room for the binding process. The painter deals daily with square feet, and the floor coverer measures in square yards. The chef measures in quarts and cups, breaks down recipes, and determines costs.

If you are going to succeed in any of the trades, math will be the single most important class to take.

Some trades require more than basic math. An electrician must understand algebra. A land surveyor needs geometry and will learn even more advanced math. A sheet metal mechanic must someday master trigonometry. So don't skip those math classes. Work hard at them.

Physical education is important, too. An electrician has to dig an occasional ditch. Being a carpenter can be like doing eight hours a day of calisthenics. A printer has to lift 30 to 40 pounds of paper at a time. There are few crafts that don't involve a degree of physical exertion. They're often downright hard work. So even if you're not particularly interested in sports, do be concerned about keeping your body fit for work.

It is safe to assume that most students who are thinking about the skilled trades as a career will be taking all the industrial arts shop courses that they can work into their schedules. If you can make time for them, there are other classes that can add to and enrich your school career. You might find room for these classes by attending summer school or taking more than the regulation six periods per semester.

Art classes can be a good elective. Art can provide an opportunity to think in terms of space, shape, and perspective. A carpenter someday turned house-remodeler can benefit from a sense of the whole. A chef can learn combinations of colors that are pleasing to the eye. House painters are encouraged to take art.

Another class that can be important is accounting. The

major cause of failure of small businesses is poor accounting procedures. If your long-term dream is to become self-employed —a contractor, plumbing shop operator, television repairman—visit your school's business education department long enough to learn the basics of accounting. It will pay off.

Students not headed for college seldom take foreign language courses. Ed Belman, a forty-year-old businessman, has decided that was a mistake.

"A lot of my employees speak only Spanish," says Belman, whose business is in southern California. "I'm taking a night class in conversational Spanish so that I can communicate directly with my own people."

French is the language of the culinary arts, so future chefs are encouraged to take at least some of that language. And if your motive for becoming a chef is the opportunity to travel worldwide, then additional languages will be helpful.

Science is usually a requirement for high-school graduation. Although there are no doubt easier science courses, physics is the most valuable for plumbers (hydraulics), office machine repairmen (force), and electronic technicians and electricians (electricity). Chemistry would be a better selection for printers, cement finishers, and painters. Biology and physiology are appropriate for future embalmers.

Let's see what a four-year class schedule would look like for someone working toward a future career as a craftsman. School districts vary, but it is assumed that three years of English and social studies are required, plus one year each of math and science, in order to graduate. Physical education is required each semester.

9th Grade
Physical Education *
English *
Social Studies *

10th Grade
Physical Education *
English *
Social Studies *

9th Grade
Math *
Drafting or Blueprint Reading
Shop

10th Grade
Algebra
Shop
Shop

11th Grade
Physical Education *
English *
Social Studies *
Science *
Shop
Shop

12th Grade
Physical Education *
Shop
Shop
Math-Science
Work Experience

Drafting is recommended because it will help the student understand spatial relationships. Not only is that a real part of the work of most craftsmen, but it is also a significant part of the test requirements for entry into many apprenticeable trades.

Work Experience is an opportunity to gain on-the-job experience and get credit for high-school classes. Most schools offer this elective. Usually the student has to find his own job and gain the cooperation of his supervisor to complete the necessary paperwork to meet the requirements of the school district. The student should make an effort to find a job related to his career goals, even if he is only doing errand-boy chores.

Young women may have a special problem. They are sometimes nervous about shop classes and their all-male population.

Susie is a good example of what can happen.

She arrived in the counselor's office the second day of school announcing loudly, "I'm the only girl in metal shop! How could you do that to me?"

"Would you like to change classes?" asked the counselor.

"Yes!"

So Susie's schedule was changed to Home Economics. The

* It is assumed that these classes are required for graduation.

counselor did not bother to point out that Susie might well be losing her opportunity for a $6-an-hour apprentice job and instead be qualifying for a $2-an-hour waitress position.

Sure it's hard to be the only girl in class, at first. In time, the students and the teacher will begin to think of you as "just one of the boys." And since a girl is probably highly motivated if she sticks it out, she is likely to be better than at least some of the boys in the class. It's likely that in time the boys will be coming to her for help. Don't let "being the only girl" scare you away from any class that interests you.

The same can be said for young men interested in futures as chefs or tailors. If you are a serious student in any field, the laughter doesn't last long.

Perhaps you think you want to be a craftsman but want to hold on to your option to attend a four-year college. That means you'll have to add geometry, another science class, and a language, while taking fewer shop classes.

There is one other chore for you while you are in school. You must develop good work habits. That means that you get to school and class on time. You don't stay home because the weather is bad or the surf is up. You do your assignments carefully and completely.

Your future employer doesn't have time for people who can't be relied upon, who aren't there or don't complete their work. Now is the time to establish the good habits that will help you throughout your life.

And after high school?

By the time you have completed all of the above courses, you will have gained enough skill in your trade to be immediately employable either as an apprentice or as a helper. You will also be eligible to attend a trade school or community college to continue your specialized training. You have a good future.

Chapter **III**

Life-style of an Apprentice

Don's * viewpoint:

"I guess you could say I'm pretty proud of being a craftsman. I've pretty well got it made. In less than six months, I'll have my journeyman's ticket and I'll be able to work anywhere in the world.

"It hasn't been an easy four years but it's been worth all the trouble. I'm only twenty-six, and I've got a wife and son and a new baby on the way. We're buying our own house, and we've got money in the bank. Oh, we're not rich, but we've got just about everything a guy could ask for.

"I remember back in high school my folks kept telling me that I ought to go to college. My grades were O.K. in algebra, geometry, and science, but I didn't like studying very much.

"Every chance I had I took a shop class. I took auto shop, electronics, machine shop, woodworking. All that stuff.

"When I graduated I knew I didn't want to go on to college, but I didn't know for sure what I wanted to do.

"That summer, I got on my bike and rode almost clear across the country. I gave myself plenty of time to think.

"By the time I got back, I knew that I wanted to have a trade, some kind of skill that was high-paying and almost always in demand.

"Then the hard part came—finding a job. I knocked on a lot of doors and asked a lot of questions. I got told "No" a lot of times.

---

* Don is not a real apprentice but a composite of all apprentices in Los Angeles, Tampa, or Jersey City who are proud of their work and their skills.

"I had to have some sort of income while I was looking for a chance to learn a skill, so I got a job selling at a lumberyard. I figured I might learn something and maybe meet someone who could help me.

"That's how it worked out, too. I got to know one of the contractors real good. He said if I could pass the tests he'd take me on as an apprentice.

"The test wasn't too hard. A lot of math and those spatial relations things.

"Right from the beginning I was making good money, 60 percent of the journeyman's rate. And every six months I got a 5 percent raise.

"On the job, I worked and worked really hard. Most of the time a journeyman I was working with would teach me how to do something. Or maybe the boss would come around and show me something new.

"And two nights a week I had to go to class. We got to practice on equipment that maybe we weren't using on the job. And we got into the theory of electronics and control circuits, blueprint reading, things like that. The classes weren't all that hard, but two nights a week for four years, even with summers and Christmas vacation off, gets to be a drag. You can bet my wife will be glad when I'm done."

Joy's viewpoint:

"It *has* been a long four years. It's hard having Don out two nights a week. And there have been a couple of times when Don was laid off between jobs and had to draw unemployment benefits. I wasn't too sure we'd be able to pay the bills, but we made it.

"I've kept working most of the time so we could buy things for the house. After this baby is born, I'd like to stay home for a while with the children. Baby-sitting is pretty expensive for two children and I'd just as soon stay home, maybe do some painting around the house. I'd like to re-cover our old rocking chair, too.

"Don's father helped us with the down payment for this house. We'll pay him back, but it will take a while. It's not exactly a mansion, but Don has done a great job fixing it up.

"He's already remodeled the bathroom and kitchen. Now we're adding a new room for the baby and an extra bath. It just seems like Don can do everything around the house. I'm really very proud of him."

Don's future:

"I've thought maybe someday I'd be a contractor myself. You know, be on my own and hire other people to do the work. I don't know, though; that would take a lot of capital.

"Sometimes, Joy and I talk about moving to a small town, maybe up north. I'd be able to find work easy enough, and the cost of living would be less. A small town might be nice for the kids. But we kind of hate to leave our folks behind, and all of our friends.

"Even if I just stay as a journeyman here, the future looks pretty good.

"We don't have to worry about medical expenses or retirement. The union contract is really good. I have to pay union dues every month, but that buys me medical insurance and life insurance, and the contractors have to put money into a vacation fund and a retirement program. And the union makes sure my hourly pay rate keeps up with inflation.

"As soon as the house is all fixed up and I have a little more spare time, I'd like to ride my bike more often, or even buy a bigger one. Maybe I could enter some up-hill races. I used to do that and really enjoyed it. Joy and the kids might learn to like it, too.

"Yeah, I'm glad I went to the trouble of becoming an apprentice. It's a good life."

Chapter IV

Women in Apprenticeable Careers

Marylou grew up fixing things.

When she was little, she was far more interested in building block castles than playing with dolls, unless the doll needed to be fixed.

She turned wagon wheels into go-cart wheels, and she fixed the flats on her bicycle without asking for help.

Marylou installed her first electrical system when she was fourteen—a light for her closet. It may not have looked particularly professional, but it was electrically correct and it lit up her closet quite adequately.

In high school, Marylou took a typing class because everyone said typing was important for a girl to know. But she found the typing chair uncomfortable and the practice letters deadly dull. She got an "A" in the course, though, because the teacher found that Marylou could make a broken typewriter work when others couldn't.

Wood shop was more fun for Marylou. Of course, she was the only girl in the class, which meant she took a lot of teasing from her classmates. But the teacher didn't laugh. Marylou was fully as talented as the boys in the class and more serious about her work. She made an end table for her bedroom. The top, carefully finished to a satin sheen, was an inlaid checkerboard design.

Algebra and geometry were probably Marylou's best academic subjects, but she didn't really enjoy studying all that much. She wasn't enthusiastic about going to college at all.

High-school graduation arrived, and still Marylou had no career goal. A summer job at a hamburger stand gave her a little income, but it wasn't very challenging and had no real future.

And then Marylou's boyfriend, Mark, told her about the test he was about to take for a job as an apprentice electrician. Marylou asked a lot of questions. Would they accept women? Was the test hard? What did you have to know to pass it?

Mark didn't have many of the answers, but he did know the telephone number of the union office.

A call to the union confirmed the fact that applications were being accepted for future apprentice electrician openings. And, yes, women were both acceptable and encouraged to apply.

By 1975, when Marylou was searching for a career, affirmative action programs supervised by both the federal and state governments required apprenticeship programs to actively recruit and enroll a quota of females as well as members of minority racial groups. Most of the unions were having great difficulty finding young women who were both qualified and interested.

"The test wasn't too hard," recalls Marylou. "There was a lot of math, mostly basic stuff. And there was a lot on spatial relations where you have to look at a drawing of the front of a bunch of squares and tell how many there are all together."

Marylou was one of 12 females out of 1,200 applicants who took the test. She and 5 other women passed.

"About three months later, I had to go in for an interview," says Marylou. "A panel of about six guys asked me all sorts of questions. They wanted to know why I wanted to be an electrician, what experience I had, and stuff like that. They gave me kind of a hard time about being female. They weren't at all sure I could handle the heavy work. I just told them that I figured I could dig a ditch if I had to and I really didn't mind getting my hands dirty."

The interviewing panel accepted Marylou, and her name went on the eligible list. She was one of the first of this group to be hired, since the union was anxious to fill its quota of female apprentices.

The union hiring hall referred her to her first job.

"I was really scared that first time," recalls Marylou. "I didn't know how the men on the job would react, and in all honesty, I didn't really know if I could do the work. Of course, the first thing they did was hand me a shovel and tell me to dig a twenty-foot ditch about two feet deep. Man, was that hard work! But I did it.

"It took the boss a couple of days to decide that I was really there to stay. Then they started giving me some other jobs to do. Nothing very complicated, of course, because I was a first-period apprentice, but at least it wasn't such hard physical work.

"It seems like every time I go out to a new job they put me through the same routine. Dig a few ditches or do the hot, sweaty crawling around under the house. When they see I can hang in there, they treat me pretty much like any other apprentice.

"Sometimes there are guys on the job that resent women. They hassle me about sex, and their language can really be foul. I either laugh it off or ignore them, and pretty soon they ease up.

"It's a good job. The pay is great, the work interesting, and I like not being stuck in an office all day."

Marylou is looking forward to being a highly skilled, well-paid journeyman electrician.

Not every girl is interested in a career that requires quite as much physical strength as electrician, carpenter, or plumber. But young women who have a natural mechanical aptitude can have considerable success in a variety of apprenticeable skilled trades that offer a secure future and high pay and require only average physical strength.

Women are having success as office machine repairmen, meat

cutters, electronic technicians, and in the printing trades. None of these jobs requires the physical strength of jobs in the construction industry. They do, however, require mechanical aptitude, and most of them require ability to work with numbers.

Office machine repairmen need enough strength to lift a typewriter, but every secretary has had to do that. Ability to diagnose a mechanical or electrical trouble and correct it is more important on this job than is physical strength. That all-important first job is often obtained after taking trade-school courses and gaining some practical, salable knowledge.

Much of the heavy lifting a meat cutter must do is aided by mechanical devices. The trays used to restock meat counters may weigh twenty to thirty pounds. Usually, these apprentice jobs are available to store employees who have been hard-working box boys or cashiers and have expressed an interest in the training.

Electronic technicians may learn their skills either in an apprentice program or through trade-school training. Aerospace firms and computer companies have been very accepting of female technicians and have been encouraged through affirmative action programs to hire women in this nontraditional job title.

The printing trades are becoming more mechanized and computerized. The result is that there is less requirement for physical strength but greater need for knowledge of modern equipment.

Other apprenticeable trades in which women will be finding more and more opportunities include auto mechanic, blacksmith, cook, jeweler, locksmith, musical instrument mechanic, optical technician, silversmith, and telephone lineman.

It's not easy for a woman to become an apprentice. But then, it's not easy for a fellow to become an apprentice, either. It takes ability, determination, hard work, and a willingness to stick with it until you find a job.

Marylou isn't the only girl in the world who doesn't mind getting her hands dirty, and she likes the paycheck that goes with skilled employment.

Chapter V

Automobile Mechanics

There was a lot of pressure on Craig to go to college. He had done well in high-school math and science. His parents and his counselors saw Craig as a future engineer.

Craig didn't see it that way.

"I tried college and it was boring," he says. "Auto mechanics is the only thing that has ever held my interest."

After dropping out of the University of Washington, Craig tried a variety of jobs. Eventually, he found himself in southern California, got a job in a gas station, and began taking auto repair night classes at Santa Monica City College.

As Craig's knowledge of auto repair increased, he also began to realize that he was underpaid at the gas station. He had a talk with the one instructor whom he admired the most.

"I just wanted to ask Mr. Knowland about how much money I should be making and where I could get a better job," recalls Craig. "Before we were through talking, Mr. Knowland had offered me a job at his garage as an apprentice."

"Craig is the kind of young man I like to hire," says Barry Knowland, for twenty-five years a garage owner specializing in hard-to-diagnose car troubles. "He is very intelligent, has a lot of natural ability, is well motivated, articulate, and wants to be a professional mechanic, not a parts changer."

Knowland has trained more than a dozen mechanics in his shop through the years. Right now, he employs Craig and one experienced mechanic full time. Three young men who have trained with Knowland work part-time in the shop when not working their regular jobs as firemen.

If Craig sticks it out for four years, he will have a guaranteed job as a journeyman mechanic in Knowland's garage. That means he will be earning $1,000 to $1,500 per month. And there is the possibility that Knowland will offer Craig a part of

Craig thinks that diagnosing a problem is the best part of his job.

the business, increasing Craig's potential earnings to $20,000 per year. Craig will also have the option of opening his own garage, if he can save sufficient money to buy the necessary equipment.

"I start new apprentices on tune-ups and electrical jobs," says Knowland, "then they move on to fuel system problems. I like them to try new things, too, with my help. I don't want them to get in over their heads, but I do think the job ought to be challenging. If I know Craig is taking the air-conditioning class and we get that kind of a problem in the shop, I'll get him to work on it.

"I teach my boys how to make repairs the right way and how to make money at it. I give them advanced books to read that they would never get in school, and I expect them to read and understand them. I teach them how to handle the public, make estimates, deal with personnel problems, handle the banking, where and when to buy merchandise, and generally be a good business manager.

"It took me ten years of saving to be able to go into business myself, and then I was in a partnership. It was another six years before I could afford to be on my own."

Knowland estimates that it takes $50,000 to open a properly equipped garage.

"Some guys try to open a garage without buying the proper equipment," he says; "then they simply can't do a good job, and they go out of business because the customers don't like the work."

Like all mechanics, Craig already has an investment in tools. So far, he has spent $1,400 on hand tools, and he expects to spend several thousand more. One wrench, which he may use only once a month, cost $25. But the job can't be done without the correct tools. The problem, and the cost, is compounded in the United States because of the need for both metric- and English-sized tools.

Craig continues to go to school two nights a week. He hopes to earn a vocational diploma, which requires the completion of forty credits in auto mechanics. Knowland is his class instructor.

Both Craig and Knowland are convinced that the most important classes a high-school student can take, if he wants to be an auto mechanic, are physics, chemistry, and electronics.

Says Knowland, "The air-conditioning system is all based on physics, the transmission is hydraulics. If you want to really understand the car and be able to diagnose a problem, not just change parts until the thing works, you have to understand the laws of science that are involved."

"Diagnosing a problem is the best thing about the job," says Craig. "It's the hardest part, but it's also the most creative."

Math and geometry are also important in repair work, but not as critical as the sciences.

As an instructor of auto mechanics, Knowland often finds himself in a position to refer his students to job openings.

"Sometimes I call up a friend in the business to tell him about one of my students who is ready for a job," he says. "Or sometimes they call me if they are looking for someone who is particularly good at air conditioning or transmissions. I'm really happy to help out my 'A' students."

Of course, not all the students are as talented as Craig. Some have a lot of natural ability and can put together a transmission without understanding all of the hydraulics involved. Those students, in time, will make excellent general mechanics and will surpass students only able to change parts, good ones for bad ones. Other students understand the sciences involved but lack the mechanical ability to make a piece of equipment work.

The auto repair industry offers stable employment. There are seldom layoffs, and the demand for auto repair actually increases during times of recession when consumers choose not to buy new cars but to have the old ones fixed.

Mechanics must be happy with greasy hands and clothes. Often they work in half-open buildings that lack air conditioning and can be cold during the winter months. The roar of motors racing and the hammering of air compressor-operated tools are common.

Craig and Knowland share a mutual enthusiasm for becoming a total mechanic. "If you're a good mechanic, you can work anywhere in the world!"

SOME FACTS

In 1974 more than 700,000 auto mechanics were employed in the United States. It is anticipated that 22,300 new mechanics must be trained each year to keep up with the increasing demand for auto service through 1985. This means that well-trained auto mechanics will be able to find jobs easily through at least the 1980's.

In addition to training as a general mechanic like Craig, it is possible to specialize in a particular repair field. Specialists earn somewhat less money than would an all-around mechanic.

Automatic transmission specialist—must understand gear trains, couplings, and pumps.
Tune-up specialist—must understand ignition systems, timing, valves, and spark plugs.
Front-end specialist—must align and balance wheels, repair steering and suspension systems.
Brake specialist—must adjust, replace, or repair linings and hydraulic cylinders.
Radiator specialist—must locate and solder leaks, clean with caustic solution.
Glass specialist—must replace broken glass and repair operating mechanisms.

Mechanics may work on commission or on a straight salary. In Knowland's small garage, he prefers that his mechanics work on salary to help maintain a "family" atmosphere where they can help each other on difficult jobs. In larger shops, a good, fast mechanic may benefit financially by working on commission.

In 1974 the average hourly pay for mechanics in the U.S. was $7.02.

Some areas of the country, such as northern California, are highly unionized in the auto repair industry. Formal apprenticeship programs are more frequent in unionized areas than elsewhere.

Dealers provide their own factory-sponsored training for their mechanics. The trainee becomes familiar with only one type of car, however, rather than learning about a variety of products.

The 1970's saw an occasional female enter the trade as an apprentice, but for the most part the auto repair industry remains a man's world.

RELATED CAREERS

Auto body and fender repair is also an apprenticeable trade. In 1972 some 161,000 persons were employed in the trade, twice as many as during World War II. About 4,100 new auto body repairmen will be needed per year through 1985.

Auto body repairmen use special machines to align damaged frames and body sections. They remove damaged body sections with pneumatic metal cutting guns or acetylene torches and weld in new sections. They must know how to push large dents out with a hydraulic jack or a hand prying bar. They use plastic or solder to fill small dents and then file the repaired area smooth. Some body repairmen also do their own painting, though another specialist is often employed for this task.

The apprenticeship period is most often three years.

Some mechanics specialize in truck and bus repair. In 1972 there were 130,000 such specialists, with 5,100 new job openings anticipated each year.

CLASSROOM WORK

Craig is involved in an informal apprenticeship agreement, and his boss expects him to attend classes two nights a week until he completes all of the available auto repair classes. Were Craig in a state or union-supervised apprenticeship, he would be required to attend 144 hours of classroom instruction per year during the four years of his apprenticeship.

Course content varies slightly, but the following suggests a general description of auto mechanic and related courses available at a typical vocational college:

Automotive Mechanics Courses. Welding, use of hand tools, and principles and repair of engines, electric systems, drive train components, suspensions, steering, braking, tune-up, carburetion, transmissions, wheel and axle alignment, emission control systems, air conditioning, brakes, and finally engine rebuilding. In all cases, the appropriate math and physics involved are emphasized.

Truck and Heavy Equipment Repair Courses. Courses are similar to those for automotive mechanics with the addition of information about diesel engines and fuel systems.

Auto Body and Fender Courses. Welding, brazing, soldering, fender repair and replacement, chassis straightening, estimating, and painting.

Courses may also be available in motorcycle repair and auto servicing, though apprenticeship programs are seldom available in these areas.

Chapter VI

Chefs

Travel, travel, travel.

A desire to travel plus a deep love for elegant cooking are the motives the apprentice chefs at Los Angeles Trade College talk about when they speak of the skills they are learning. They talk with admiration of their friends, recent apprentice graduates, who are now working in Hawaii or Oslo, Norway. Many of the eleven apprentices in the class hope to turn their skill as chefs into passports to unusual places.

Ingrid Cark dreams of further study in Switzerland in her pastry specialty. The fact that she speaks some Dutch, Spanish, and French will help her with the transition.

"Almost half of the apprentices in Europe are women," says Ingrid, "so I shouldn't have any trouble getting a job. There are Hilton Hotels (her current employer) all over the world, so I could stay with them and transfer wherever I want to go."

Another option open to Ingrid, after she completes the three-year apprentice program, is to work at resort areas like the Bahamas.

"I wouldn't mind working a season at a resort hotel and then traveling for a few months before I went to another resort area," says Ingrid. "The more places you work, the more you learn and the more valuable you become as a chef."

Persistence and a total commitment to her goal of becoming a qualified chef helped Ingrid become an apprentice. After high school, she worked briefly as a boat builder ("I like physical labor," she says) and as a waitress. She moved to San Francisco and managed to become a member of the Culinary Workers Union. They referred her to a job as a breakfast cook, though she had never done any cooking before. The employer agreed to try her out for two days.

With success as a breakfast cook behind her, she approached the master chef at the San Francisco Hilton to accept her as an apprentice.

"I kept calling him back and he kept putting me off," recalls Ingrid with a smile. "Finally, just before he quit his job to go somewhere else, he hired me. I guess the new chef was a little surprised to find a female apprentice on the job, but there wasn't much he could do about it."

After only six months of experience, Ingrid entered a culinary contest. Her tray of canapés on a mirror with an elaborate dough basket for a centerpiece took third place in the professional judging.

When Ingrid changes jobs, it usually takes a few days for her new co-workers to accept her.

"When they see I have the skills and the talent for the job, they respect me and even look up to me," says Ingrid. "Oh, sure, they make jokes about women, but it's all in fun. Sometimes the language gets a little rough, but that doesn't bother me. And if I come upon a group of guys telling dirty jokes, it gets quiet all of a sudden. But basically I haven't had any trouble with being accepted."

The physical demands of the job have not been difficult for Ingrid, either, though the work involves lifting heavy pans and standing for long hours. Her delicate features and slight stature suggest that the work doesn't take overwhelming strength.

"If I need help carrying something, I ask for help just as the men do," says Ingrid. "They have to worry about back problems or hernias, so we're used to helping each other. Usually it's easier to carry something myself than wait for someone to help."

In addition to her favorite pastry work, Ingrid also enjoys making soups and sauces.

"The fry station is the hardest," says Ingrid. "It really gets hot."

While in high school, Ingrid took basic home economics and enjoyed it, but finds it wasn't very useful in terms of her current work. If there had been a more advanced class, it might have been more beneficial.

Her parents, particularly her father, were very resistant to the idea that Ingrid was entering a man's world as a chef. She's glad she ignored their concern.

"Cooking is an interesting and beautiful world," she says.

Sinar Parman, also a student in the apprentice class, shares Ingrid's enthusiasm for the artistry of being a chef. His favorite task is to create a *garde-manger,* the tray of cold meats and cheeses garnished with care, often served for buffet lunches or dinners.

Sinar hasn't yet decided what he will do when he finishes his final year of apprenticeship. He is considering returning to college to get a degree in hotel management. He has already completed two and a half years of school in a psychology major. Sinar is also tempted by the lure of travel to Europe.

Sinar feels that his most important high-school classes were languages, particularly French, the basic culinary language, and basic math.

"The chef will ask you to make up a $100 cheese mirror, and you have to know how much to put into it," says Sinar. "You have to figure the average cost per pound of the cheese and know what the company policy is about the wholesale price versus what we charge the customer."

Arthur Miller, another apprentice, is twenty-seven years old, married, and has one child. He finds the long, irregular work hours difficult to manage and hard on his social and family life. It is not unusual for him to work eighteen days straight. And it's only the overtime pay that helps his family make ends meet.

"You have to really like cooking to go into the field," says Arthur. "You can't fake it when you have to work every weekend."

For five years Arthur was a cook in the Army, where he learned basic skills. "There's no vanity in the job in the service," he says. "It's just cafeteria work."

Arthur sometimes gets discouraged when he learns a new skill in class but it's a long time before he gets to try it on the job.

"They're teaching us French cooking in the class," says Arthur, "but that's not what we're really doing. Everything is so commercial now, labor-saving. Meats are precut, vegetables are frozen. Some things are precooked."

Though pastry is interesting and *garde-manger* is artistic, Arthur likes sauce-making the best. He finds the variety of spices used in Oriental and Caucasian sauces a challenge, but African cooking has caught his imagination. The special curries and dry roots used in African sauces, even though they are sometimes hard to obtain, add particular zest to a meal. Arthur would be delighted to work in a restaurant that specializes in African cuisine.

Travel doesn't tantalize Arthur as much as it does Ingrid and Sinar. He is planning to work a while in Hawaii after he finishes his apprenticeship. Eventually, he would like to have a civil service job as a health inspector.

"The pay is pretty good and the hours would be regular," says Arthur.

Arthur has invested $200 of his own money in tools. There are special knives for each task like garnishes or cutting sandwiches, and each knife costs $18 to $25. "If you want the right tool, you have to buy it yourself," he says.

David Hedley, the class instructor, agrees with Arthur that apprentice pay rates are too low and the hours of work are too long and irregular. Like many chefs in this country, Hedley was trained in the European apprenticeship program. Chefs thirty years his senior and current apprentices in Europe have all received identical training.

"The apprentice program here in Los Angeles is not too good," says Hedley, "but they are trying to improve it. I know in the San Francisco area the union is stronger and their apprentice program has been in operation longer."

About three out of every fifty students Hedley teaches have the qualities to make a really top chef.

"You have to enjoy food and preparing it," says Hedley. "You have to be willing to work irregular hours that interfere with your social life. You have to be able to put up with lots of pressure and have an even temperament. You have to be intelligent and diplomatic.

"On the brighter side, chefs have a marvelous opportunity for travel. They can work in hotels anywhere in the world, or for shipping lines or places like the Alaska pipeline. A café fry cook just doesn't have that kind of opportunity."

Chef training can also lead to nonkitchen jobs. Chefs have become teachers, hotel managers, salesmen of food products or kitchen equipment, and supervisors of food services in hospitals. These jobs offer more regular hours and pay well.

Hedley's students are likely to have the most trouble with basic math problems. "In my class of forty-five day students, nine failed a simple math test. They have to be able to convert recipes, measure portions, and figure in pints and quarts." (Hedley thinks they will be changing over to the metric system within a few years.)

He finds knowledge of French important if a young person is planning to work in a first-class establishment.

"A young person should try to get an apprentice job in the best class hotel he can find," says Hedley. "In a hotel, you can learn all three meals plus banquets. At a dinner house, you can't get the same variety of experience. It's helpful if you can work for a chain hotel. That way you can change locations and stay with the same company."

SOME FACTS

In 1974 about 955,000 cooks and chefs were employed in the United States in restaurants, schools, colleges, hospitals, government agencies, factories, and private clubs. It is estimated that 52,000 new cooks and chefs must be trained each year through the 1980's to meet the growing demand.

The food service industry is the nation's third-largest industry and the fastest-growing. It is estimated that the average American eats one out of every three meals away from home. The industry provides 750 million meals a week through more than 367,000 individual establishments, and new food service operations are opened every day. (Fast-food outlets and vending-machine foods are the fastest-growing portions of the industry.)

The role of chef has been changing in recent years. A creative spirit is still required, but now the chef must be an organizer, personnel man, and buyer. He must have knowledge of nutrition and diet. He may have to lay out and design a kitchen. He will have to calculate and control both food and labor costs to show a profit.

Pay rates for chef in 1974 ranged from $3 to $5.90 per hour, depending upon the geographic location and type of establishment.

Apprentices generally start at 65 percent of the journeyman's rate, with regular increases. Chefs with a national reputation may earn $40,000 per year.

Modern facilities are generally air-conditioned, which has improved the general working conditions for chefs. Some of the work remains hot and involves long periods of standing and an ability to lift heavy pots.

High-school students interested in this career field are encouraged to master basic math, including the conversion of pints and quarts, percentages and fractions. French is the basic language of the culinary arts, and high-school study of the language will be useful. Basic home economics classes do not usually teach the gourmet techniques that are used by chefs. Advanced classes would be more beneficial.

CLASSROOM WORK

In Los Angeles, apprentices attend class one afternoon a week for the three years of their training. The class is strictly a lecture and involves no demonstrations or actual practice. (This may vary from program to program.)

The students learn about the history of culinary art, organization and administration of a professional kitchen, flow of work from station to station, and safety. They gain a knowledge of the merchandise including meats, fish, vegetables, fruits, pastas, pastry, dairy products, cheeses, beverages, spices and herbs, and convenience foods. They learn the basic requirements for preparation of soups, fish, eggs, meat, poultry, and game.

Students must also learn to select and store food, use leftovers, determine size of portions, plan menus, and buy food in quantity.

Sanitation and public health rules are discussed in the classroom.

Chapter VII

Carpenters

The Carpenter's Training Center in North Hollywood is part of a big warehouse building. There are four classrooms and a workshop large enough to build a one-room, fifteen-foot-high practice house. Apprentice carpenters come to this building one or two nights a week during the four years of their apprenticeship.

Evan Jouliane, Lin Duke, and Fidel Ramirez all attend on Thursday nights, though they are in different classes.

Evan, twenty-three, is about half way through the apprenticeship program. Before he officially enrolled as an apprentice, he was working as a construction laborer at a mountain resort area three hundred miles from Los Angeles.

"I worked on a lot of jobs, mostly building condominiums," recalls Evan. "The jobs were nonunion, so sometimes I'd tell them I was an apprentice to get the work. I learned a lot about the construction business, laying steel and framing, and I finally decided I'd try to get a journeyman's ticket."

Evan's father knew a contractor in the Los Angeles area. The contractor, after interviewing Evan, agreed to hire him. The contractor gave him a letter to the union saying that Evan had a job as an apprentice waiting for him. The union accepted Evan's $50 initiation fee, told him where to attend night classes, and Evan became a first-period apprentice.

(Note: Apprentice carpenters complete one period of training every six months until they finish a total of eight periods.)

Evan has worked quite steadily for this same contractor for the last two years. Only during 1975, when new construction was very slow, did Evan have to draw unemployment benefits, and then only for one month.

"Occasionally we're laid off for one or two days between jobs," says Evan, "but the work has been pretty regular."

Since Evan has a wife and daughter to support, he is concerned about steady income. Evan's wife is quite happy about his learning the carpenter's trade. It makes him handy at fixing things around the house, and he has made quite a bit of their furniture.

"You have to work hard at being a carpenter or you're not going to make it," says Evan. "I've had some friends talk me into recommending them for a job. First, they're scared of getting dirty. Then they get lazy and start goofing off. They get fired in a week."

Harry Ashcraft, Evan's night class instructor, feels that Evan has the makings of a good carpenter.

"He takes pride in his work," says Ashcraft. "He's the kind who can walk by a building and say, 'Hey, I helped to build that—looks good, doesn't it?' He also has the basic math skills necessary to do the work. Algebra and geometry aren't important, but a carpenter does have to add, subtract, multiply, divide, and work with fractions."

Lin, twenty-eight, is one of the few female carpenter apprentices in the Los Angeles area, and these last two years have not been easy for her.

"I had been going to college taking anthropology, psychology, and things like that," recalls Lin. "None of it seemed to make sense. I finally decided to get back to basics and learn a trade. All I knew about was carpenters, electricians, and plumbers. I picked carpenters."

First, she called the carpenters' union. They told her the date and place for the next apprenticeship test.

"I got some books out of the library so I could brush up on my math," says Lin. "That part of the test went O.K., but they had a section on tool identification. I didn't know a hammer from a saw."

Nonetheless, Lin passed the test with a grade over the required minimum of 70 percent. Then the waiting began. She

Lin is one of the few female carpenter apprentices in Los Angeles.

was told that her name had been placed on a waiting list, but that only a few apprentices were given the right to go job-hunting at a time, so the area would not be flooded with new apprentices. Months went by.

"Finally, I went to talk to the union business agent," says Lin. "I had been living on $2-an-hour part-time jobs just waiting to be an apprentice. I was mad and I was desperate. Just one call from the business agent to the joint apprenticeship committee (the group that supervises the testing and training of apprentices), and I had my 'hunting license' so I could look for a job."

Lin's troubles were not over.

Apprentices can report for early morning roll call at the union hiring hall in the hope that some contractor will call in requesting an apprentice. But that seldom happens in the carpentry trade.

Most apprentice carpenters must find their jobs by contacting contractors directly.

"I used the yellow pages of the telephone book and called whole pages of contractors," recalls Lin, understandably bitter. "I got one interview and no jobs."

Again she went to the union business agent for help. He helped her land a job, finally, with a contractor building a freeway. Since government construction contracts require employers to hire minority-group personnel, and women qualify as a minority, the freeway contractor was more willing to hire a female apprentice than other contractors had been.

"I have never worked so hard in my life," says Lin. "It was like eight hours of calisthenics every day. I thought I wouldn't make it through those first two weeks."

Lin worked a year on the freeway job. She has had one other job lasting a month. During her two years as an apprentice, she has worked a total of thirteen months. She continues to pay her $20-a-month union dues and attend the apprentice night classes so that she can qualify for unemployment benefits as an apprentice.

While Lin worked, she had to become accustomed to derogatory remarks made by the men about herself and other women. She thinks the older men, particularly, feel threatened by the presence of a woman carpenter. In the classroom, with the young men apprentices, she is usually ignored.

Lin doesn't consider the night classes difficult at all. The study manual has the tests printed in them, so all she has to do is memorize the answers in order to pass the required tests every six months. The classes are supposed to meet from 6:30 to 9:30, but often her classes are released about 8:00. She is also taking a college-level architectural drawing class, which is helping her to understand the total picture of how a building is constructed.

Lin isn't very optimistic about her future as a female in a man's occupation in a man's world. She and her roommate, Diana, also a carpenter apprentice, hope to start their own construction firm to serve the needs of the women's community. Two other small groups of woman in the area are trying to do the same thing, making competition for such jobs already tight.

In Lin's experience, the only successful female carpenters have been women whose husbands have died, leaving the wife with a going contractor's business.

Because of affirmative action programs, unions must accept qualified females as apprentices. Employers are still, however, reluctant to hire a woman. For a woman to succeed as a carpenter, she will probably need solid connections in the industry until she can establish herself as a competent craftsman.

Fidel, twenty-seven, has experienced some feelings of prejudice against him during the three years he has been an apprentice, but on the whole he has had good foremen to work for and good relationships with his co-workers.

Fidel left his home in Durango, Mexico, to move to the United States. Like immigrants before him, he was seeking a better life. He was a high-school graduate but spoke little English. Once in Los Angeles, he was able to find intermittent work as a construction laborer. He wasn't able to see much of a future for himself, his wife, or his three children.

Finally, Fidel got a break. He was able to enroll in a federally-funded program to pretrain carpenters in the East Los Angeles community, an area populated primarily with Mexican-Americans. The month-long course, for which Fidel was paid, provided him with enough knowledge to pass the apprenticeship test.

About two weeks after he took the test, Fidel had his "hunting license."

It took him two more weeks to find a job. He applied at thirty to forty construction sites before a foreman finally said

Fidel gets "hands-on" experience during apprentice night class.

yes. The job was thirty miles from home, but Fidel was on his way, finally, to a well-paying job.

Fidel is very proud of his trade. He has had to draw some unemployment benefits during the last three years, but never for long. Each year, the jobs are easier to find, since he has become a good framer and is always a hard worker.

Like most of the apprentices, he has invested $150 to $200 in the hand tools required for the trade.

He continues to improve himself and his chances for steady

employment by taking an English class one night a week.
Fidel is happy about his future.

Testing for apprentice carpenters occurs on a fairly regular basis throughout the year, depending in part on the level of construction activity in the area and the need for new apprentices. Information about testing dates can be obtained by calling any local office of the carpenters union. That office will refer the call to the appropriate joint apprenticeship committee office.

Applicants are required, in the Los Angeles area, to be eighteen and a high-school graduate, or to have passed the equivalent GED test. There is no maximum age limit.

The apprentice test involves basic math problems and some algebra and geometry, reading comprehension, and spatial relationships.

Those applicants who achieve the 70 percent passing mark are placed on one of several waiting lists. Because the carpenters' apprenticeship program is highly structured and carefully supervised by state and federal officials, it must have an affirmative action program. The effect of the affirmative action program is to give preference in the hiring of minority-group applicants through the use of quotas.

To qualify as a minority-group member and therefore to get his name on the shorter list, the applicant must identify himself in one of the minority classifications. For instance, if a person is as little as 1/16th American Indian, he can be considered a minority applicant for purposes of the affirmative action program—but only if he checks the square marked American Indian.

According to a union representative, "We don't pressure the applicants in any way about their ancestry. They have to identify themselves."

Unfortunately, a person of Mexican-American ancestry who does not have a Spanish surname does not qualify as a minority applicant.

SOME FACTS

In 1974 about 1,060,000 carpenters were employed in the United States. It is anticipated that 37,000 new carpenters must be trained each year to keep up with the demand in the construction industry. This means that skilled carpenters have a secure future through the 1980's, although most carpenters will experience some periods of unemployment between jobs or due to seasonal layoffs.

Of all the construction workers, the skilled carpenter is most likely, because of his overall knowledge, to become the general foreman or to become self-employed as a general contractor.

Most carpenters are employed by contractors and homebuilders, but a substantial number are employed in remodeling projects, for government agencies or utilities, or as maintenance carpenters in manufacturing plants, hotels, or large office buildings. Carpenters are also employed in the shipbuilding, mining, and sign and billboard industries.

The pay rate in 1972 for a journeyman ranged from $6.57 per hour in Denver to $9.45 in Cleveland. Nationwide, the average in 1974 was $8.41 per hour. Normally, apprentices start at 50 percent of the journeyman's wage and receive a 5 percent increase every six months.

Some carpenters are self-employed. They "bid" a job for a contractor for a flat rate. They must learn to bid in a way that gives them a profit. The faster they can complete the job, the higher their equivalent hourly pay becomes.

Recommended high-school classes for students interested in carpentry and related occupations include basic math, wood shop, blueprint reading, and drafting.

RELATED CAREERS

Roofer, floor-covering installer, and cabinetmaker are also apprenticeable trades.

In 1974 about 90,000 roofers were employed, most of them working for contractors. The apprenticeship period is three years. Apprentices start at 65 percent of the journeyman rates. Journeymen earn an average of $8.10 per hour. (See Chapter XX.)

Floor-covering installers install, replace, and repair floor coverings of resilient tile, linoleum, vinyl sheet, and carpeting. In 1974 some 85,000 floor-covering installers were employed by either contractors or retail stores. Often an installer specializes in one type of covering. Apprenticeship programs are usually three to four years, but many installers learn on the job as helpers. Pay rates range from $5.50 to $8.00 per hour. (See Chapter X.)

Some workers classified as cabinetmakers are really semiskilled employees, required only to assemble precut parts. A skilled journeyman cabinetmaker makes custom-designed items with the emphasis on quality and craftsmanship.

A large manufacturer of household cabinets, church, and commercial fixtures is likely to be unionized. The small custom furniture manufacturer is less likely to have union employees. Where a union is not present, apprenticeship programs are likely to be quite informal.

CLASSROOM WORK

Carpentry Courses. In the classroom, future carpenters learn the use of hand and machine tools, basic math, blueprint reading, and how to estimate job costs. They learn about forms, foundations, concrete, framing, interior and exterior finishing, stair building, remodeling, and the appropriate building codes.

Cabinetmaking Courses. The student cabinetmaker learns blueprint reading, layout, math, the use of hand and power tools, and finally cabinet construction and millwork.

Apprentices normally attend class one or more nights a week for a total of 144 hours of classroom training per year. Attendance is required, and excessive absences may result in the apprentice's being dropped from the program. This requirement appears to be enforced somewhat inconsistently.

"Most of the students do their homework and get something out of the class," says one instructor, "but there are others whose attitudes are really poor. They shouldn't be allowed to just float along, not doing their part."

Chapter VIII

Electricians

The twenty-five fourth-year apprentice electricians work quietly at the long tabletop desks. They are taking a 190-question test on electrical codes and theory in preparation for their professional exam coming up soon.

In the adjoining room, third-year students learn about control panel circuits by wiring sample boards.

Two nights a week for four years, apprentice electricians attend classes at Long Beach City College. If they fail to attend regularly, they may not get their automatic pay raises on their daytime jobs, or they may even be dropped from the apprentice program.

Morris Cross, twenty-eight, married with two children, will soon have his journeyman's ticket.

Ed Marek, twenty-eight and single, has one more year to go.

"It was two years from the time I applied to be an apprentice 'til I started," recalls Morris. "I was working as a machinist, but I wanted the higher pay scale that electricians make."

Morris had also been taking classes at a trade school while working full time. It was his instructor who told him when the electricians' union was accepting applications.

It took Ed even longer to get his name on the list of apprentices, even though his father is an electrician.

"I applied three times before I got on the list," says Ed, "and then I made it only because the list was extended for a second year."

While waiting for his name to come up on the list, Ed worked in a grocery store as a box boy and checker. He also has an Associate of Arts degree in data processing but was unable to find work in that field.

Both Morris and Ed find the installation of control panels for motors the most challenging and interesting part of their work.

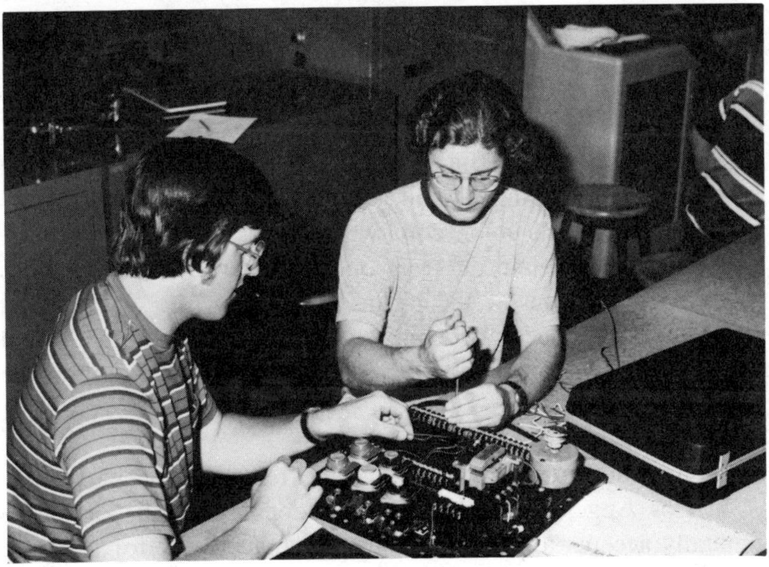

Ed (right) and a classmate practice wiring a control panel.

Digging ditches, a sometimes necessary chore, they voted the worst part of the job.

During Ed's three years of training, he has had only industrial/commercial jobs. He has yet to wire a house.

Morris' wife is pleased with his job but sometimes worries about his safety. "We do have to work with high voltage and at heights," Morris explains as he shrugs off his wife's concern, "but the contractors are very safety-conscious, and so am I."

Both young men own about $90 worth of hand tools, which

represents the minimum required tool list for electricians. It is also the maximum list, since the contractors are required to furnish all other tools.

Morris thinks a high-school student interested in a future as an electrician ought to take all the industrial courses he can, such as mechanical drawing, and all of the math available. "Even algebra isn't enough," says Morris.

"I've never seen anyone use trigonometry on the job," Ed points out, "but you've got to have it to get through the theory classes."

With the exception of one month during a slow winter construction season, both Morris and Ed have had steady work. Their union dues of $30 a month entitle them to be sent out on jobs from the union hiring hall, the only place where contractors are allowed to seek union employees.

"When you get laid off from one job, there's always another job waiting for you at the hiring hall," says Ed. "It's a good career for someone who enjoys working with his hands and doesn't mind getting dirty. It's not like working in an office shuffling papers."

Competition for electrician jobs is extremely tight.

In Los Angeles County, the joint apprenticeship committee annually accepts applications only one hour a day for ten days at five different locations. Usually this occurs in August, but it may happen only every other year, depending on construction activity and how many openings for apprentices are anticipated.

"We only indenture apprentices if we are pretty sure there will be sufficient work to keep them regularly employed," says a representative of the apprenticeship committee. "All hiring is done through the hiring hall. The apprentices aren't allowed to go job-hunting themselves. We can keep pretty close track of how many apprentices we're going to need."

In 1975, 1,300 applicants filed during the limited open period. They were all age eighteen to thirty-one, had completed high school or the GED, and had taken one year of high-school algebra or equivalent.

Each applicant was required to take a standardized aptitude test, which included spatial relationships, manual dexterity, and ability to work with numbers.

And then came the long process of interviewing each applicant, a procedure that took nearly nine months to complete.

Says one interviewer, "I look for individuals who are physically capable of doing the work, who are genuinely interested in this specific field, and have a real desire to work at it."

Of the original 1,300, only 868 remained eligible after the testing and interviews. There were about 120 openings for new apprentices that year.

An eligibility list in each of the five geographic locations was established. To comply with the requirements of affirmative action, separate lists for each minority group are kept. In order to increase the number of minority-group apprentices, applicants may be accepted from the minority lists who have a lower overall score than some on the longer white male list.

Once having enrolled them in the program, the night class instructors look for students with a lot of natural curiosity about the field of electricity, stick-to-itiveness, and the ability to get along with others.

"If students are going to have trouble with the classes," says fourth-year teacher Jack Bohannon, "it's usually with homework and attendance, not with the academics. I think a kid who has been in the military and gotten some discipline and maturity, or one who has had really menial jobs and can appreciate what a skill will give him, is the most likely to get through the classes."

The dropout rate for apprentice electricians is quite low, only 5 percent statewide in California. The dropout rate for carpenters is much higher, close to 25 percent, largely because those apprentices are not guaranteed a job by their union.

In the last few years, there has been a decline in the number of electrician apprentices accepted in the Los Angeles area because of an overall decrease in construction activity. Opportunities would be greater in other areas experiencing high construction levels or would generally improve if the economic situation were more encouraging for construction.

"A construction electrician has a lot of flexibility," according to Bohannon. "He can work anywhere in the world. If he doesn't like the boss or the hours or the location, he can quit his job and go back to the hiring hall to get another one. A maintenance electrician is what we call a 'lifer.' He's locked into one job and one retirement plan working 8:00 to 5:00 the rest of his life. If he doesn't like the boss, there isn't much he can do about it."

William Sandridge, an apprentice maintenance electrician with American Can Company, disagrees. Bill sees no advantage at all to becoming a construction electrician. As a maintenance electrician, he can enjoy a variety of assignments from laying conduits to fixing motors, and he doesn't have to worry about layoffs because of bad weather or slow construction seasons.

"Wiring the electrical panels for this machinery is much more sophisticated than wiring a house," he says.

Apprentice jobs at American Can are considered promotional opportunities for their semiskilled employees. Seniority, often fifteen years with the company, is the only basis to move up to an apprentice job. Bill had waited a long time for one of the infrequent openings.

"After I get my journeyman's ticket, I think I'll go to school on my own," says Bill. "I'd like to learn about air-conditioning and heating systems. That way, I could open up my own shop after I retire."

Bill has already invested $500 in hand tools to do his current work.

All of the electrical work is enjoyable for Bill, but he finds he must also do some plumbing as part of the job. He is required to handle both water pipes and air lines and doesn't find that part of the work as interesting.

During Bill's four years as an apprentice, he will be learning about electrical installation and assembly, maintenance and repair, overhaul of motors and generators, repair of automotive and industrial truck equipment, and maintenance and repair of the main power supply. This particular plant uses city power, which is fed through transformers to increase or decrease the voltage as necessary.

Bill attends school two nights a week.

"So far, we've just been learning about DC theory," says Bill of his first year of classes. "We'll get into AC theory later."

His 144 hours of classes each year will eventually cover electrical drafting, electrical mathematics, AC and DC theory, AC and DC motor and generator theory, motor and generator repair and maintenance, controls and control circuits, elementary industrial electronics, and electrical codes.

Very few companies have a formal apprenticeship program for maintenance electricians. More often, a young man with a trade-school background will be hired as a helper and learn on the job, or the firm will hire an experienced construction electrician for the work.

SOME FACTS

In 1974 some 245,000 electricians were employed in the United States. The demand for newly trained electricians is expected to increase through the 1980's, with opportunities for 11,000 training slots each year.

Most electricians work for electrical contractors or are self-employed. A small percentage work for the government or in large businesses.

Electricians install and wire heat, light, power, air-conditioning and refrigeration equipment. They may also install electrical machinery, electronic equipment, controls, and communications equipment. They must be able to read blueprints and bend and fit conduits or plastic-covered wire. They make electrical connections by soldering or mechanical means and then test for proper connection and grounding. They must have a thorough knowledge of appropriate electrical and building codes.

As a rule, the electrician furnishes his own hand tools, including screwdrivers, pliers, knives, and hacksaws. The employer typically furnishes pipe threaders, conduit benders, test meters, ladders, and electric drills.

Electricians are the highest-paid workers in the construction industry. In 1974 the rate paid in urban areas averaged nearly $9.00 per hour.

Normal color vision is required, since wires are color-coded for easy identification and tracing.

High-school students interested in the trade are encouraged to take algebra, trigonometry, basic science, and basic electronics, if classes are available.

Although opportunities do exist for women as construction electricians, some of the work requires considerable muscle power. "Wiring a house is no problem," says one instructor, "but climbing a ladder with a heavy roll of wire or digging a 100-foot trench can be tough."

There were 280,000 maintenance electricians employed in the United States in 1974, more than the total number of construction electricians. It is anticipated that 9,800 new maintenance electricians will be needed each year through 1985 to keep up with the moderately increasing demand.

Maintenance electricians typically work for large manufacturing concerns. Their work involves keeping lighting systems, transformers, generators, and other electrical equipment in good working order. They may install new electrical equipment or repair motors and welding machines. They must know how to read blueprints and diagrams.

The average wage in 1974 was $5.64 per hour. The journeymen at American Can were earning about $7.50 per hour in 1976. Union dues averaged $15 per month, or 3 percent of their paychecks.

A small percentage of maintenance electricians are women.

CLASSROOM WORK

Electrician apprentices are required to attend classes 144 hours per year, which normally means two nights each week during the school year.

Classes include an introduction to electricity, including AC and DC theory. Practical experience is provided in wiring installation, junction boxes, terminal strips, communications equipment, and switches.

Industrial control systems are studied in order to understand manual and automatic circuits, alternating and direct speed and directional control types of pilot devices, timers, releases, relays, protective devices, starters, and safety practices.

The appropriate electrical codes for both residential and industrial applications must be mastered.

Considerable math is involved, including algebra, trigonometry, decimals, percent, proportion, and ratio.

Chapter IX

Embalmers

A funeral home is not always a somber place.

"We take our cue from the family," explains Lyn Golden, a twenty-year-old apprentice embalmer. "Some of the families have accepted the death and can talk quite freely about the deceased. Other families show their bereavement and sorrow by crying all the time. In either case, we try not to walk around with sour faces."

After trying a variety of careers including construction, sales, and a semester of Bible college, Lyn thinks he has found the right career.

"You're helping people at a very difficult moment in their lives," says Lyn. "It's a good feeling when they thank you for what you've done. They are very appreciative of your work."

Lyn became an embalmer almost by accident. He was unemployed when a friend mentioned that a local mortuary needed a "night man."

"All I had to do was answer the phones and let people into the slumber room," recalls Lyn. "After a while, the boss suggested that I apply for my apprentice license so I could learn embalming."

In California the apprentice license costs only $5 and is required before the person is even allowed in the embalming room when a body is present.

"I almost fainted once when I watched an autopsy being done," says Lyn. "Basically, you mustn't think of the body as the remains of a formerly living being. It's just a shell, almost like a doll, and my job is to preserve it properly until burial."

Lyn's job is to remove the blood from the body and replace it with embalming fluid. The abdominal cavity must be aspirated to remove gas and extra fluid, and embalming fluid injected.

Not every body is embalmed. Some religions prohibit the

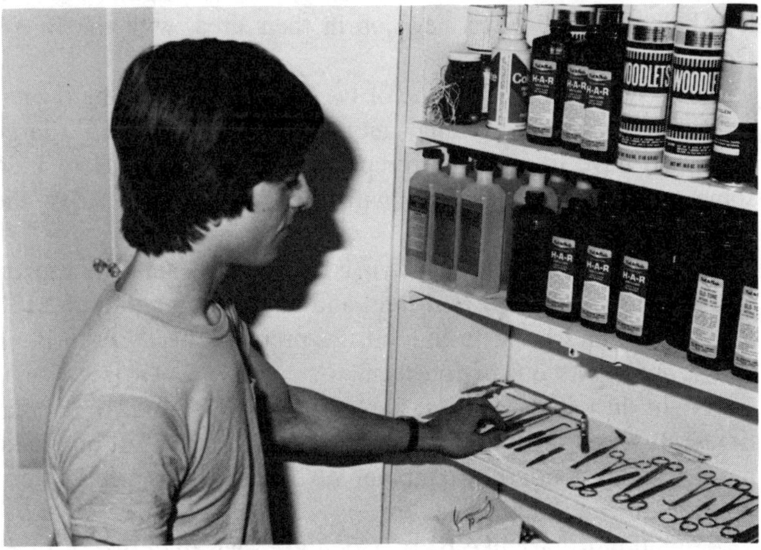

Lyn checks the embalming room supplies as part of his work as an apprentice.

practice. About one out of every ten cases is cremated, and if the cremation is immediate embalming is not required. Generally, if the body is to remain unburied for forty-eight hours, embalming is necessary.

Part of Lyn's job is to make the body look as natural as possible. He may use lip rouge and powder. If there has been an injury to the face, he may cosmetize by rebuilding a portion of the face with wax. The hair must be combed and the body dressed.

Some of this work Lyn has learned on the job. He will become more proficient while he attends nine months of mortuary college.

Like many new embalmers, Lyn has worked a year as an apprentice before enrolling in college so that he can be sure he likes the career field. Because there was no mortuary college near his first employer, he has moved to the Los Angeles area, where he will be able to attend school and work nights. The college helped Lyn find his new job in their area, with the B. W. Coon Mortuary.

At B. W. Coon, Lyn is one of two employees plus the owner.

"I like working for a small mortuary," says Lyn. "In a large place, I'd have to be in the prep room all the time. Here I do some of the gardening, help with the services, and drive the family cars."

As a full-time employee, Lyn is provided a small house on the mortuary property, rent-free, and a take-home pay of $130 a week. He and his wife live on the premises because he is on call seven nights out of fourteen.

"Night duty is the hardest part of the job," says Lyn. "Sometimes you'll get a call to pick up a case at 10 o'clock. It may take me a couple of hours to embalm it. Then I'll just get to sleep when another call comes in."

A small mortuary like B. W. Coon averages only two or three cases a week, but there are occasional weeks with many more cases to manage.

Bill Coon has owned and operated his mortuary for forty-six years, and his father owned the business before him. Like many funeral directors, Coon is quite religious, and when he hires an apprentice, religion is important to him.

"I look for young men who respect their elders," he says. "I want them to have a Christian viewpoint. I don't want them to smoke or drink or use bad language. This is a service organization. We're building personality and patience. Thinking about others and not yourself is important."

According to Coon, low entry pay rates and long hours are the principal reasons young people drop out of the apprentice program.

"They have to really start at the bottom and work their way up," he says. "They have to prove themselves before the wages improve. And not all young men are willing to be as tied down as this job requires. Someone always has to be ready to take care of a call."

The inability of a young person to cope with death on a regular basis is not usually a primary reason for dropping out of the program.

"In order to be a good embalmer, you have to take a personal interest and pride in your work," says Coon. "I want an employee to give full measure for his time and be willing to do anything necessary around the mortuary."

As an example of the pride Coon takes in his work, he always makes sure a body is prepared properly even if it is not expected to be viewed. "You just never know when a family will decide at the last minute they want to see the deceased one more time," he says.

Lyn hopes that he someday will be a funeral director and own his own mortuary.

"An embalmer can make a decent living," says Lyn, "but owning your own place is the way to really make money."

According to the industry magazine to which Lyn subscribes, the going sale price for a mortuary starts at $150,000, requiring more capital than Lyn is likely to have for a long time.

"Sometimes you can get started by buying shares," Lyn says hopefully.

After Lyn finishes his two years of apprenticeship and the nine months of full-time college, he should be able to find employment close to almost any geographic location he chooses. The number of school graduates in recent years has pretty well matched the demand for new employees, making employment prospects stable.

SOME FACTS

In 1974 there were 45,000 licensed funeral directors and embalmers in the United States. A substantial number of these are owners of their own mortuary.

Most of the 23,000 funeral homes in the United States are small, employing only one to three directors and embalmers. A few large combined cemetery-mortuaries may employ more than twenty embalmers. A few embalmers are employed by morgues and hospitals.

Licensing requirements for embalmers vary from state to state. Generally, a high-school diploma or equivalent is required, plus graduation from an accredited mortuary science school. Minimum age is twenty-one. About half of the states require a year or more of college in addition to training in mortuary science.

Embalmers prepare the body for viewing and burial, whereas the funeral director helps the family make the personal and business decisions necessary for the service and burial. One person may perform both of these services and continue to help the family after the burial with details related to social security benefits, insurance, etc.

Apprenticeship training for embalmers is two years, which must include one year of school in mortuary science. The schooling may be taken before, after, or during the on-the-job training, but most funeral directors suggest that a young person arrange to get some on-the-job training before enrolling in classes.

The personal traits required for the job include composure, tact, the ability to communicate easily, and the desire and ability to comfort others.

High-school classes recommended include biology, chemistry, and speech.

Wage rates in 1974 for apprentice embalmers ranged from $2.25 to $4.00 per hour. Housing may be provided for the apprentice in addition to the paycheck.

In 1974 funeral directors and embalmers earned between

$200 and $300 per week; a manager earned $10,000 to $15,000 per year. A mortuary owner typically earns more than $20,000 per year.

The owner or director of a mortuary often belongs to one or more community service clubs, like Lions or Kiwanis, and is frequently active in his church. Contacts made through these activities provide future customers.

There appears to be considerable resistance on the part of small mortuary owners to the hiring of female apprentices. They justify their reluctance on the basis that they require their young men to carry bodies and do manual labor around the mortuary. Larger employers whose employees can specialize are more likely to be receptive to female applicants.

Apprentices who are members of minority racial groups tend to be employed by mortuaries that serve the minority communities.

For a list of accredited schools, write to: American Board of Funeral Service Education, Inc., 201 Columbia Street, Fairmont, Virginia 26554.

CLASSROOM WORK

Twenty-eight schools are accredited by the American Board of Funeral Service Education, Inc., to offer mortuary science courses. About half of these schools are private vocational colleges offering a one-year program. In the classroom, students study anatomy, physiology, embalming techniques, restorative art, psychology, accounting, and funeral law.

A small number of colleges and universities offer two- and four-year programs. Students in these programs take liberal arts and management classes, in addition to mortuary science courses.

Chapter **X**

Floor Coverers

Brian Burke, twenty-three, already has the telltale bump on his kneecap that is the badge of a carpet layer.

Three years as an apprentice in the trade has given Brian the bump, strong arm muscles from lifting 400- to 600-pound rolls of carpet, and, as a new journeyman in the Los Angeles area, a wage of $9.50 per hour.

"I'm glad I got into the business when I did," says Brian. "I was hired because I had worked some summers and weekends for my boss as a helper. He knew I'd work hard. Now to get the job, I'd have to go through the union, and they are only sending out blacks because of the affirmative action stuff."

Brian's boss has been extremely resentful of the affirmative action programs and very hesitant to hire minority-group employees. Like many of the union shops in the area, he doesn't plan to hire any more apprentices for some time.

The construction activity in the Los Angeles area has been slow in recent years, leaving fewer opportunities for new people in the trade. A few years ago there were 400 registered apprentices in floor covering in the Los Angeles area. By 1976 there were only 100 active apprentices, with 250 on the waiting list. The union does not administer a screening test, but it does interview each applicant.

The floor-covering industry is not highly unionized. Less than half of the companies in Los Angeles are union shops. In some areas of the United States, the percentage is even smaller.

Most of the retail establishments are operated on a family basis, with two brothers or a father and son laying the carpet, linoleum, and soft tile, and mama doing the bookkeeping.

To land that first job with a family-operated business, you need to have connections (an uncle or friend in the trade) or you will have to convince an employer that you really want to learn this particular skill.

"I think if I were entering the trade now," says Bruce Adams, an instructor in apprentice-level courses, "I'd look for a job as a material handler. That's the flunky, entry-level work. Then I'd hope the mechanic I was working with would like me well enough to teach me some of the skills."

Adams feels that the most important asset an apprentice can have is dependability.

"A customer is told he is going to get his new carpet on a certain day at a certain time," says Adams. "That probably means the customer has moved a lot of furniture out of the way to get ready for the carpet. And if the carpet doesn't show up on time, he can really get upset. I've seen more apprentices get fired because they were unreliable than for any other reason."

When Adams hires a new apprentice, he looks for someone who is not afraid to work hard.

"If they have been around the trade and know it's heavy, hard work, there's usually no problem," he says. "If they're just after the money, they won't last."

Adams also looks for people who have good hand-eye coordination, can handle math problems involving square yards, can measure carefully and read blueprints.

Other employers may be particularly concerned with the steady work history of an applicant.

"I'd rather hire someone who has been a box boy for two years at the same place," says one employer, "than somebody who has never worked more than two weeks on any job, even if he does have some experience in the trade."

Since not all employers furnish trucks for their apprentices, an applicant needs his own reliable transportation. Sometimes the day's work may be fifty miles from home.

When Brian started as an apprentice, he helped rip up old carpeting and put down the tackless strips for the installation of the new. He learned to use the hot seaming tape to connect the joints of the carpet, then stretch the carpet smoothly into place.

"It's really just a question of learning how to handle the different kinds of carpet or linoleum," says Brian. "You have to know what glues to use on what kind of floors for linoleum or tile. Layout is like working a jigsaw puzzle. You've got to cover the most floor with the least amount of yardage."

Adams feels that the highest-skilled floor coverers are those who can do linoleum coving which involves forming the linoleum up the wall a few inches to eliminate cracks and corners. "That's why the boss doesn't let me go when work gets slow," says Adams. "It's just too hard to find guys who can do the coving."

Although Brian has done some coving, he doesn't consider himself an expert yet.

Sometimes a particular job offers a real challenge.

"The cement finishers don't always do their job right," according to Adams. "If the floor is uneven, you can't just lay tile on it, so we have to mix a floor fill that will set up fast. When we get it level, then we lay the tile." The technique is called "floating the floor."

Brian is thinking about opening his own shop some day. "It would take a lot of capital," says Brian, "but I think being your own boss is the way to go."

SOME FACTS

In 1974 about 85,000 floor-covering installers were employed in the United States. It is anticipated that 3,200 new installers will be needed each year through 1985.

Experienced floor coverers earned between $5.65 and $7.90 per hour in 1974.

Installers cover floors, walls, countertops, and other surfaces with carpet, linoleum, or soft tile of composition, cork, rubber, metal, or plastic. They must measure, cut, and fit the material, taking special care to match patterns.

The materials are usually installed over wood or concrete floors, and the installer must inspect the floors to see that the floor is dry, smooth, and free of dirt. The installer may sand, paint, or even resurface floors.

The new covering must be attached to the floor with appropriate adhesive material or tackless strips.

The employee is normally required to furnish his own hand tools, which may mean an investment of about $40. The tools include knives, cement spreaders, scribers, rollers, carpet stretchers, straightedges, and measuring tapes.

Back and knee injuries are common in the industry.

Most installers are employed by flooring contractors or by retailers, usually in urban areas.

High-school courses recommended for students interested in the trade include mathematics through geometry, wood and metal shop, mechanical drawing, and blueprint reading.

Apprentices in formal union programs attend classes one night a week during their three to three-and-a-half years of training.

Very few women have entered the trade, primarily because of the heavy lifting involved and employer resistance to hiring them.

Chapter XI

Land Surveyors

Algebra, geometry, and trigonometry are the tools of the trade for land surveyors, and that's part of why Ed Rinaldo likes the work.

"I had been a construction laborer for about four years before I got into this apprentice program," says Ed. "It got so that I really hated to go to work even though I was making about $7 an hour. I used to watch the surveyors at work. They were using their heads and not a shovel. I took a $2-an-hour cut in pay to start as a surveyor, but in the long run I'll make a lot more than I would as a laborer."

Surveying work also appeals to Ed because he can be outdoors all day and doesn't have to go to the same office or plant or even surveying site each day.

In high school, Ed took algebra but not geometry or trigonometry. Two years ago, he began taking surveying courses at a community college. It was those classes that gave Ed enough math background so that he could pass the qualifying test to become an apprentice land surveyor. About a third of that test, as Ed recalls it, was algebra and two-thirds geometry. Unlike most other apprentice-qualifying tests, there were no sections on reading comprehension or spatial relations.

Ed is very pleased that he landed a job with a small surveying company after he passed the test and was eligible to search out his own job. His company tries to maintain a steady employment level, accepting just enough subcontracts from developers to use the same number of crews almost year-round so that it doesn't have to lay off any of its employees.

Ed thinks the current project will last nearly two years. They have just finished the staking for rough-grading a housing tract of 3,000 homes in Orange County, California. He will have to drive the thirty-seven miles from his home to that tract many more times before all the surveying steps are completed.

Ed appreciates what a responsible job he has as a surveyor, and how even more responsible the position will be when he becomes chief of party, the leadman of a three-man surveying crew.

"My first week on the job, the boss fired a long-time chief of party," recalls Ed. "The chief hadn't checked to make sure just where a sewer line came in, and the construction crew dug a twelve-foot trench three feet to the wrong side of the hole. That error cost 'em plenty, and they fired him."

Ed doesn't think of himself as being good at math.

"There's a lot I don't get in class as fast as some of the other guys," says Ed, "but when you go out and actually do it, it suddenly makes sense."

Steve Basoco, another first-year apprentice in Ed's class, never showed a lot of promise in math, either. It took him three years to complete Algebra I in high school.

"I guess it took me a long time to mature," says Steve, now twenty-seven years old, married, and a father. "I've had fifty-one jobs in the last ten years, and I've been in trouble with the law. Now I feel like I really know where I'm going, and I'm glad I have a chance to get there."

Steve doesn't recall either the union or management representatives asking him any questions about his police record. "They just didn't seem concerned," he says.

When Steve completed the application form to become an apprentice, the joint apprenticeship committee gave him an outline of the test he would have to take.

Fortunately, both Steve's father and uncle are surveyors. With their help, Steve crammed enough algebra and geometry into his head to pass the test.

"Even if I had had geometry in high school, I don't think I would have retained it well enough to pass the test without studying," says Steve.

After Steve passed the test, his uncle hired him to work for his small surveying firm. That meant Steve had to join the union. There was a $300 initiation fee, which could be paid off $100 at a time for three months. Monthly dues are $13.

Steve has worked for several employers in the area and has experienced very little unemployment during his first year of apprenticeship. The possibility of layoff does worry him, however.

Steve, like Ed, likes surveying because it is an outdoor job. "It doesn't have the same kind of pressure that a factory job has," he says.

Paul Detilla is the same age as Steve, twenty-seven, but is a fourth-year apprentice and already acts as chief of party.

Paul had completed three years of college as a biology major before he entered the apprentice program. He had hoped to work for the Fish and Game Department, but found there were few openings and the pay would be much lower than he could make as a surveyor, his father's occupation. Fortunately, the joint apprenticeship committee gave Paul credit for some of his college course work and for his years of helping his father on the job. He is moving through the program faster than the average apprentice.

Paul has found the most difficult part of the apprentice class work, and also the most interesting part, to be the astronomy sessions. Although surveyors seldom have to determine boundaries by sighting the sun or stars, they must at least learn the procedures. The only time they might have to use this system is if they are in a wilderness area and can't tie their lines into a known boundary. And then a computer would aid their work.

All of the apprentices have invested some money in their own tools. Although the employer is required to furnish most of the equipment, the apprentices have each purchased $45 to $65 worth themselves. A good scientific pocket calculator is a necessity for the chief of party and usually for a head lineman.

Ed, Steve, and Paul attend classes two nights a week, which they find does cut into their recreational time.

Ed finds he is putting on a little weight since he is no longer doing heavy laborer's work to use up the calories. He has joined a health club so he can work out regularly.

Steve is a poet and a published songwriter. His first song, "Reflections of Your Smile," has been recorded in Hollywood as a love song and will soon be recorded in Nashville as a country-western.

Paul spends his spare time, when he has any, sailing a flying junior racer, a small dinghy-size sailboat. He hasn't won any races, but he still enjoys the ocean.

What causes one person to succeed as a surveyor and another to drop out of the program?

"I think success is a combination of good leadership ability, academic skill, and manipulative ability," says Edgar Milstead, administrator of the joint apprenticeship committee for surveyors in the greater Los Angeles area. "If an apprentice fails, it's usually because he is not 'work wise.' He doesn't know how to give a full day's work or can't stand the pressure from the chief of party to get the work done. A few of the apprentices can't handle the math, but we test for that before they enter the program, so that's not usually the problem. We do have a high dropout rate when construction is slow and employment is poor. If we can't get them a job, they can't usually survive."

The Los Angeles apprenticeship program is unique to the industry. In most parts of the country, trade or vocational schools provide the training for new surveyors, and beginners work their way up through the ranks to chainman, senior chainman, and eventually chief of party.

Not all surveyors become chief of party. Some do not want the added responsibility that goes with the job. Others are not sufficiently qualified to handle the more difficult work.

The chief of party must supervise the work of the three-member team. He has to be able to use good judgment and get the job done more efficiently than his competitors might. Accuracy and speed are important. A surveying error can be very expensive to correct.

The Los Angeles program is five years. During four of those years, the students attend classes two nights a week. A few apprentices, like Paul Detilla, become chief of party before they complete the full term of apprenticeship. However, before they can become a certified chief of party and licensed to hire their own people, they must complete all of the course work and have at least six months' experience as a chief of party.

In recent years, the opportunities for women and members of minority racial groups have improved in the surveyor's portion of the operating engineers union (as they have also for operating engineers).

There are a few young women in the apprentice program, but they haven't yet set the world on fire, according to Milstead.

"We would really like to attract high-caliber young women and young men of minority racial backgrounds," he says. "We think they can do the work if they are well qualified, but it's sometimes a problem, particularly with women, to get them interested in the job."

Milstead does feel that surveying is a physically demanding job. A surveyor must dig holes, tramp over rough terrain, use an eight-pound sledgehammer, and be exposed to the dangers of poison oak, rattlesnakes, and working near heavy equipment or on a busy street in the midst of traffic.

Although the employers are trying to cooperate and will hire women, a female can expect some prejudice on the job and some static from her co-workers.

"If she can do the work, she'll be all right," says Milstead.

SOME FACTS

In 1974 about 55,000 surveyors were employed in the United States, less than 5 percent of them women. Of the 55,000 surveyors, 20,000 are registered as licensed chief of party.

The demand for surveyors is expected to increase moderately through the 1980's, with an estimated 2,700 newly trained surveyors needed each year through that period.

About one-third of the surveyors work for government agencies such as the Bureau of Land Management, the Forest Service, or state and local highway departments. Others work in the construction industry for engineering companies or for petroleum, natural gas, or public utility firms.

A few surveyors accept temporary overseas assignments of two years, usually with oil companies. The pay rates are exceptionally high, but the job usually involves working seven days a week for many months at a time. Not many surveyors sign up for a second hitch, according to one instructor in the field.

Surveyors locate land boundaries and prepare maps and legal descriptions for deeds, leases, or other documents. For a topographic survey, the surveyors determine elevations, depressions, contours, and location of distinguishing features such as buildings, roads, and rivers.

The tools used for this task include a theodolite (to determine altitude), a steel tape or surveyor's chain, a level rod, and a range pole. A surveyor may have to clear brush away in order to accomplish his work.

Several steps are required to complete the surveying of a construction project. In the case of a residential subdivision, for instance, the first surveying step is to make a topographic map. From that map the developer is able to determine the feasibility of the project and anticipated land preparation costs.

Then the surveyors return to the project to stake for rough grading. After the grading is accomplished, the surveyors stake the street lines. The surveyors must return again to the construction site to stake for sewers and stake for the rough grade of the individual home lots.

Two more trips to the construction site are needed. The surveyors must stake for curbs and finally for lot lines when they tie down their control points, so that future homeowner disagreements about fences and overhanging trees can be legally resolved.

In 1974 a chief of party employed by the federal government earned from $9,500 to $13,000 per year. A rod worker, the entry-level job, started at $6,000 per year.

In 1976, in the Los Angeles area, the starting apprentice wage was $5.62 per hour, the chainman earned $9.89 per hour, and the chief of party earned $11.24 per hour. These pay rates seem quite high, but keep in mind that in the construction industry you can anticipate a certain amount of unemployment because of weather conditions and slow building activity. Chainmen and apprentices are likely to experience the most unemployment.

High-school students interested in becoming surveyors are encouraged to take algebra, geometry, trigonometry, calculus, drafting, and mechanical drawing.

An ability to visualize objects, distances, and sizes is considered important to the job. Normal hearing and eyesight are required.

CLASSROOM WORK

Much of the classroom work is centered around problem-solving, with the emphasis on the use of algebra, geometry, and trigonometry. Differential calculus is learned to the extent necessary to solve area problems of land with irregular boundaries, such as a river on one side of the property.

Students also learn the laws governing surveys and how to write legal deed descriptions.

Chapter XII

Locksmiths

Although locksmithing is not usually thought of as an apprenticeable trade, Carol Salisbury says, "You never stop learning."

Carol landed her job with a mobile locksmith because she knew the owner.

"I knew I didn't want to work in an office all day," says Carol. "I persuaded him to at least give me a try."

Carol hadn't had any high-school shop classes, so working with tools was new to her. "I was afraid at first even to use the drill," she recalls. "It's really easy now. I don't know what I was scared of."

Mechanical ability and a good memory are important to a locksmith.

"Every lock comes apart differently," explains Carol. "If you can't remember how a particular brand of lock works, you can waste a lot of time on the job. Sometimes you come across a lock that you're not familiar with, and then you have to figure it out on your own based on other locks you've worked on."

Carol spends most of her time changing combination locks or installing new ones. Sometimes a call comes in on her radio-dispatched truck to go to a business firm that has recently fired an employee and wants all of its locks changed. She gets many calls from motorists who have locked themselves out of their cars—a $20 job that requires about a minute of Carol's time.

She also gets calls to make a master key system for apartment houses or businesses. The master key must open all the doors while individual keys open only a specific door.

A few jobs Carol and her partner turn down. "We won't change keys on some of the late-model cars," she says. "It involves taking the whole ignition apart, and we don't have the tools to do it easily. We suggest they take the car back to the dealer."

The only problem Carol has had as a female in the trade is that she will not go out alone on night calls. Her male partner has responsibility for night emergency jobs.

To keep up with changes in the trade, Carol reads the monthly trade magazine and attends annual conventions in the area where lock manufacturers demonstrate their new products.

Carol suggests that a young person interested in the work go to a locksmith shop and ask to hang around awhile to see what the work is like. "It's more than just picking locks," she says.

Only a few schools offer classes in locksmithing, and she does not recommend the currently available correspondence courses. "You have to have someone show you how to do it," she says. The only way to land a job is to keep asking locksmiths if they have any openings. Beginning pay rates are generally minimum wage.

Locksmithing requires very little capital to go into business for yourself. Carol estimates that $1,000 can start a business. The largest expense is getting an ad in the yellow pages of the telephone directory. "Almost all of our calls are emergencies, and the people all look in the yellow pages," says Carol.

"The best part about this job is that every day is different," says Carol. "When you arrive in the morning you never know what kind of job you may have to do. I like that."

SOME FACTS

In 1974 some 9,000 locksmiths were employed in the United States. Most locksmiths are employed in small shops. Others work for the government, large industrial plants, or manufacturers of locks and safes.

Pay rates for an experienced locksmith range from $4.00 to $6.50 per hour, with trainees starting at minimum wage. A self-employed locksmith may make more than the above hourly wage.

Locksmiths typically work forty to forty-eight hours per week and may be on call at night.

It is expected that the demand for locksmiths will increase somewhat through the 1980's as the population becomes more security-conscious.

Locksmiths pick locks, duplicate keys, and open combination locks. Rekeying a master system is considered the most complicated task generally done by a locksmith.

Locksmiths are familiar with the use of screwdrivers, pliers, tweezers, electric drills, lock picks, and key-cutting machines.

Mechanical aptitude, good eye-hand coordination, and manual dexterity are requirements of the job. Often the work involves public contact, so a neat appearance and tactful personality are important. Applicants should have no criminal record.

Recommended high-school classes include machine shop, mechanical drawing, and basic math.

Locksmithing is considered one of the cleaner mechanical trades. Most locksmiths are outdoors often, as they drive from one job to another.

Chapter XIII

Machinists

High overhead, rows of finished cans move along conveyor belts. Stamping and metal-pressing machines roar so loudly that all the factory employees must wear company-issued white earplugs. Even visitors to the area are issued pink, wax-coated cotton balls to be worn as temporary earplugs.

In the room adjoining the factory space, Robert Bisbee works as an apprentice machinist. An occasional scream of metal against metal can be heard above the background noise of the factory and routine machine shop activities. Casual conversation is difficult except in the office space nearby.

The apprentice jobs at American Can Company are considered promotional opportunities for their semiskilled employees. Because of the union contract, seniority, often more than fifteen years, is the only real basis for landing one of these jobs. Robert had been a press mechanic, stamping out ends of cans, before this opening as a machinist occurred a year ago. He took the job even though there was no immediate increase in pay.

"This gives me a chance to learn a trade that I can work at anywhere," says Robert. "Even after I retire, I can open up a machine shop and earn a little money."

Robert has already invested $400 in hand tools for the job. He'll probably spend a total of about $1,000 in the next few years as he builds up his stock of tools.

Robert landed his first job with American Can when the state employment office referred him to a swing-shift opening at the Carson, California, plant.

"Most of our new employees now are referred by relatives who work here," says the employment interviewer, Sharon Mack. "We don't have many openings for entry-level jobs, so we don't like to advertise. Our starting pay rates are about $6 per hour in the machine assembly department."

American Can does not require its employees to be high-school graduates, though most of their young applicants have completed school. "We look for attitude and appearance, and we check the applicant's references," says Ms. Mack. "We want to avoid people who have an absenteeism problem."

During Robert's four years as an apprentice, he will learn to operate a drill press, shaper and planer, lathe, vertical and horizontal milling machines, and grinding machines. He will also learn tool and die maintenance, heat treating, and welding.

"Welding has been really hard for me so far," says Robert, "but I haven't had too much practice yet. I'm looking for a class to take at an occupational center or vocational school."

As part of the apprentice program, Robert attends a local junior college two days a week for three hours, on company time. He is currently taking blueprint reading and technical math.

Keith Chantler, foreman of the shop, says new machinists have the most difficulty learning to work with the different kinds of materials. In this shop, machinists need to operate on stainless steel, blue steel, soft steel, cast iron, aluminum, and brass. Each material requires different techniques, like changing the chuck speed, to machine them properly.

The machinists in this shop are often referred to as maintenance machinists, since they make replacement parts for broken factory equipment. They must machine the new parts to within .0005 inch of the required size.

"It helps if a new machinist can already read micrometers, gages, and blueprints before he comes into the shop," says Chantler. He also thinks attitude toward work is important.

"My machinists have to use their heads on the job. There isn't a foreman right there to tell them what to do," he says. "And they have to learn from their mistakes."

According to Chantler, his most skilled machinists are men who have spent five to seven years working in job shops, learning a variety of tasks very well.

"They treat you like dirt in some of the job shops," says Chantler. "They'll put you on a milling machine doing one job for months, and don't pay you much. But when you're done, you really know how to do the job. Then you get laid off and go some place where maybe they want you to work on a lathe. And that's all you do. After a few years of that, you can call yourself a really good machinist."

Ten of Chantler's top machinists are classified as tool and die makers, a higher pay grade than straight machinist. According to American Can's union contract, a journeyman machinist may become a tool and die maker by being an apprentice for one additional year beyond the machinist training program. Seniority is again the factor that determines who has this additional opportunity.

SOME FACTS

In 1974 there were 335,000 all-round machinists in the United States, plus 170,000 tool and die makers. Demand for machinists is expected to increase moderately. It is estimated that 13,100 newly trained machinists will be needed each year to keep up with this demand.

Most of the machinists are employed in the industrialized states of New York, Pennsylvania, New Jersey, Ohio, Illinois, Michigan, and California.

The task of a machinist is to set up, operate, maintain, and repair power-driven equipment for the cutting and shaping of metal.

Machinists must learn to operate lathes, drills, boring and milling machines, and grinders, as well as use hand tools such as files and chisels. They must be able to measure with micrometers, verniers, calipers, dial indicators, and other optical measuring instruments.

Many industries employ machinists in production or limited production activities. Machinery manufacturers, the auto industry, and producers of metal products are the primary employers. Other machinists may work for railroads, chemical manufacturers, food-processing and textile industries, navy yards, and the aerospace industry.

The work requires an ability to concentrate. Tolerances of .0001 inch must be held on critical products in the aerospace industry, with slightly lesser requirements in other manufacturing settings.

Safety is of regular concern for the machinists. It is not unusual to meet an experienced machinist who is missing part of a finger. Safety glasses, short-sleeved shirts, and protective shoes are standard equipment for the machinist. No neckties are worn.

Although some machinists learn their trade on the job, the more secure route to a well-rounded skill is through apprenticeship training.

The apprenticeship program is typically four years or 8,000 hours of shop time. In addition, apprentices attend classes for 570 hours, which may or may not be on company-paid time.

The average pay range in 1974 varied from $4.04 per hour in Greenville, South Carolina, to $6.46 per hour in Detroit. The journeymen machinists at American Can Company, in 1976, were earning about $7.50 per hour.

Apprentices start at about 60 percent of the journeyman's rate and receive regular increases.

Fringe benefits at the larger companies typically include vacation, health insurance, and retirement plans.

There is usually extra pay for employees who must work swing or graveyard shifts.

Although Chantler did not feel that a background in math was important for his machinists, most authorities feel that high-school algebra, geometry, and trigonometry are useful for future machinists. They also encourage students to take physics, chemistry, machine shop, and mechanical drawing classes.

According to federal law, an individual must be at least eighteen years of age in order to work around or with dangerous power equipment.

General mechanical ability is important for a machinist, as well as above-average intelligence and manual dexterity.

Skilled machinists have an opportunity to move up to higher-paid jobs as experimental machinists, model makers, or instrument makers. These positions require an ability to work well alone or with a minimum amount of supervision. The machinists may work directly with engineers or from only rough drawings.

There are also opportunities to become a supervisor or to become self-employed.

Increasingly, machinists are being asked to operate numerically controlled machines, which are machines that respond to the directions programmed into them through punched cards or taped instructions. Although the skill level of the machinist is less, the product is more accurate than ever before.

CLASSROOM WORK

Apprentice machinists spend much of their classroom time learning math concepts, including algebra, geometry, and trigonometry. They also must learn blueprint reading and nomenclature and basic physics of force, motion, work, power, energy, torque, properties of heat and matter, principles of light, optics, electronics, and electricity.

Advanced apprentices take a course covering the types and characteristics of materials used in machine shop work and the machining processes that control them. Types of metals, heat treating, metal working, material stresses, and exotic metal machining are included in that course.

(See Chapter XIX, "Tool and Die Makers.")

Chapter XIV

Meat Cutters

The meat-cutting room is a noticeably cool 55°. The tile floor is well scrubbed, though a few bits and pieces of meat dropped during the day's work remain to be picked up. And there is the combined smell of fish, poultry, and red meats.

Food preparation is one of the basic necessities of any society, and that is one of the reasons Shawn Tomiyasu became a meat cutter apprentice.

"My parents always told me that if you have a trade that provides food, clothing, or shelter for others—the basic necessities of life—you'd always have a job," says Shawn.

Shawn takes pride in his work and looks forward to his career.

"When you're young, you have to learn everything you can about your trade," says Shawn. "Then when you're older and your strength runs out, you'll be able to do the mental work like ordering meat and supervising the department."

"Shawn is an exceptional young man," says the store manager, Don Nani. "He has drive and desire. If he's in doubt about something, he checks with the meat manager. He's good with the customers at the front counter. He's always trying to learn something new."

Shawn worked briefly as an apprentice cook with a coffee shop chain before spending six months on active duty with the Naval Air Reserve. Upon his release from active duty, he landed a job with a supermarket chain, first as a box boy and then as a clerk-helper.

"Most of our apprentices are first clerk-helpers," says Nani. "We get a notice from central personnel that so many apprentice openings exist. Then we refer the names of any of our people who have expressed a desire to move up through the meat department."

The apprenticeship period is two years for meat cutter. During those two years, Shawn must attend night classes at a community college one night a week.

Shawn must restock the meat counter hourly at his high-volume store.

"We learn how to cut meats, how long you can store meat, what to do with poultry and fish, and how to smoke meat," says Shawn. "We have to know something about cooking meat, too. Customers need advice about how to prepare certain cuts of meat or what cuts can be substituted for others."

Shawn feels one of the fringe benefits of the job is learning about nutrition and good eating.

Shawn thinks of his work as potentially quite hazardous.

"When you're working with power equipment, you have to be serious," says Shawn. "You can't allow yourself any distractions."

One of Shawn's precautions is to own and wear safety shoes, which he purchased himself.

Shawn's work keeps him standing all day. He moves frequently from the cutting room to the cooler, which is kept at close to 32°, to the meat counter where the temperature is close to 70°.

The meat counter must be restocked at least every hour in this high-volume store. That involves lifting trays of meat or poultry that weigh between twenty and thirty pounds.

Shawn's shift varies from day to day. In order for the store to serve customers from 9 A.M. to 9 P.M., one group of meat cutters must work a 7 A.M. to 3 P.M. shift, and a second group 2 P.M. to 10 P.M.

Shawn will probably work three to four years in this particular store and then be transferred to another suburban store a few miles away.

"Employees tend to get in a rut if they stay in one store too long," says Nani. "We move them around so they can bring new ideas and new enthusiasm to the job."

Shawn's hourly rate as a journeyman will be $6.88 per hour (1975 Los Angeles union scale). A good many meat cutters supplement their income by working their regular forty-hour week for one chain and holding a part-time job with another chain store. Assigned overtime is unusual these days for supermarket employees.

Shawn can look forward to a future as the manager of a meat department. In the structure of a grocery store, that will put him just below the store manager and on a par with the produce and delicatessen department heads. A few meat department managers become store managers, but that is not the usual promotion route.

Shawn is a bit of a philosopher. As an instructor in the martial arts, his hobby since he was thirteen years old, Shawn is knowledgeable about both Eastern and Western philosophies. "Make an effort to do it right," has become Shawn's motto for daily life and work.

SOME FACTS

In 1974 there were 200,000 meat cutters in the United States. It is anticipated that 4,400 new meat cutters must be trained each year to replace retiring workers or those who terminate their employment for other reasons.

Central cutting of meat, which is then sent to retail stores, is expected to limit the growth of the trade.

Ninety percent of meat cutters work in retail stores, which means there is a demand for the trade in almost every city and town. Some meat cutters work in the wholesale industry. A very few work for institutions like hospitals, restaurants, and hotels.

Meat cutters must learn to identify various cuts and grades of meat, the proper use of tools, and how to cut and prepare fish and poultry, roll and tie roasts, grind hamburger, and prepare sausage.

Knowledge of inventory control, buying and grading of meat, and recordkeeping becomes important as a meat cutter enters management.

High-school math is recommended for future meat cutters. An applicant should have good manual dexterity and depth perception, normal color vision, and an ability to work standing all day.

Neat appearance and the absence of any contagious disease, such as tuberculosis, are necessary requirements of the job.

The 1974 pay rates for journeymen ranged from \$4.70 to \$6.80 per hour. Apprentices normally start at 65 to 70 percent of the journeyman rate and receive increases every six months.

Meat cutters employed in large cities typically belong to either the Amalgamated Meat Cutters and Butcher Workmen

Union or the Retail Clerks Union. Union fringe benefits usually include night-shift premium and extra pay for holiday and Sunday work, six to nine paid holidays per year, and paid vacations. Medical and dental insurance, paid sick leave, and pension plans are typical benefits.

Although the proportion of meat cutters who are female remains small, it does appear to be a trade in which females can succeed. The possibility of part-time employment after the journeyman rating is achieved may make the trade particularly attractive to the young woman interested in combining marriage with some high-paying incidental employment. Meat cutter pay rates are well above those received by grocery checkers and meat wrappers, more common jobs for females in the industry.

RELATED CAREERS

Some communities may have limited opportunities for apprentices in these related trades: sausage makers, slaughterhouse butchers, fish butchers, picklemen, and meat jobbers.

CLASSROOM WORK

The meat cutter apprentice must learn to identify and grade meat; break half and quarter carcasses into primary cuts such as chuck, round, loin, plate, and rib; and cut those into basic retail portions such as roasts, steaks, and chops.

Students learn the use of the following hand tools: boning knives, steak knives, cleavers, handsaws, tool-sharpening equipment, and sanitation equipment.

They also work with the following power equipment: band saws, power block saws, meat grinding and sausage slicing machines, cube steak machines, steak patty machines, and automatic or semi-automatic wrapping machines to package meat for display.

Chapter XV

Office Machine Repairmen

"It's really a sales job," according to John Feimer of the Los Angeles School District Maintenance Department. "Trouble is the name of the game. A typewriter only breaks down when someone is using it, and usually they're in a hurry for some job. The repairman has to convince the customer that he is there to help and can do something for that customer."

Feimer's department is responsible for the maintenance and repair of 40,000 typewriters, most of them in the typing classrooms in junior and senior high schools. In addition, an assortment of reproduction machines—fluid duplicators, mimeographs, thermo copiers, electrostatic copiers, and stencil machines—are repaired at the central downtown facility.

There are fifty employees in the machine repair department. Almost half are typewriter technicians, including two apprentices. There are also specialists in cash registers, scientific equipment (microscopes, balances, scales), sewing machines, general business machines, computer terminals, and reproduction equipment.

Predictably, summer is a busy time for the repair of school machines.

"Every day, we trade fifty overhauled typewriters at a school for fifty more that need annual maintenance," says Feimer. "The men deliver the good typewriters and bring back the bad. We take apart the old machines and give them a chemical bath. Then the journeymen go over the machines and put them back together again.

The next day we get fifty more machines to work on."

When electric typewriters are involved, the process is different. It takes one man a full eight-hour shift to overhaul an electric machine.

The repairmen working for the school district must know how to rcpair a widc varicty of machincs.

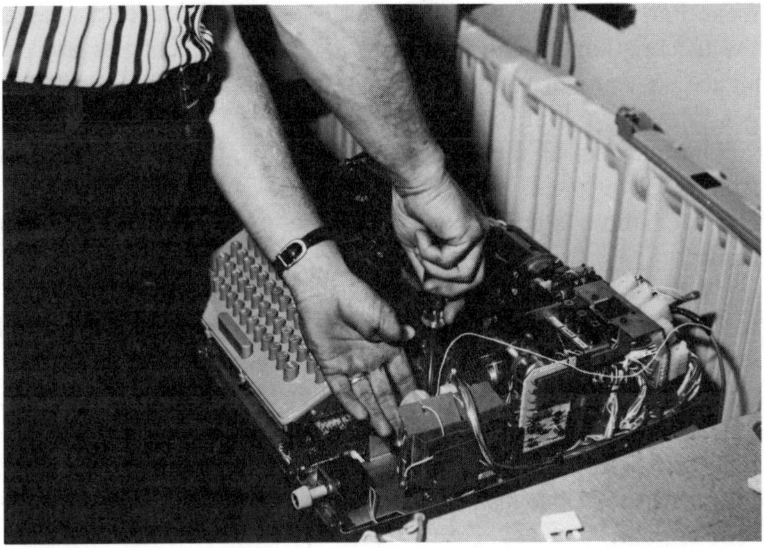

Typewriter repair is considered one of the cleanest apprenticeable trades.

"To be hired as a journeyman here," says Feimer, "these fellows have to know how to fix at least three different kinds of machines. If you work directly for a manufacturer, they only train you on their own line of equipment, plus maybe IBM typewriters since those are so popular."

Feimer expects future apprentices who are hired by the school district to be selected by competitive examination, with preference shown to minority employees. "We'll only have limited openings, maybe two every few years," he says.

To enter private industry, a young person should be willing to accept a job delivering ribbons and washing typewriters. Office machine repair is not a unionized industry. Most apprentices land a job first with a repair shop and, through showing their willingness to work and learn on their own, are later indentured.

In the Los Angeles area, the Central City Occupational Center is one of the few schools to teach office machine repair.

"If I were a young person interested in the industry," says Gene Parker, owner of his own service shop, "I'd take classes at the Occupational Center, at least at night. The courses are designed so you can progress at your own speed. Then I'd try to get a daytime job at some shop around town."

The teachers at the Occupational Center often receive calls from employers seeking new and talented employees. The teachers refer those students who seem to be serious about their career.

"When I hire a new employee," says Parker, "I look for personality, honesty, and appearance. We're particularly careful about things like body odor. You can imagine how upset a secretary would be to have a sweaty, smelly repairman come into the office. We give all of our applicants a written mechanical aptitude test before we hire them. If a new employee fails on the job, it's usually because he lacks mechanical ability or his attitude is poor.

"If the employee is talented, we'll send him to the manufacturer's schools for training on special machines.

"One of our biggest problems with repairmen is that they can't write up a service report legibly," says Parker.

Although neither Feimer nor Parker currently employ any female repairmen, they have both supervised women and find the work quite within the physical capacity of most women.

Increasingly, the new office equipment is electronic rather than just mechanical.

"If a kid has a good background in electronics," says Feimer, "either from school or from military training, he can catch on to the mechanical end of the job. But without basic electronics, there are a lot of new machines a man just couldn't repair."

Feimer believes a high-school student interested in the industry should take classes in electricity, electronics, and machine shop. Physics would help the student understand the fundamentals of levers, an important part of typewriter action. Basic math is a necessity.

"The industry wage rates don't seem very high ($5.00 to $6.00 per hour in 1976)," says Parker, "but you can't really compare them to a craft like carpentry. The work is steady, and we're never laid off for rain or snow or strikes."

A young person starting out in the industry may travel in several directions.

If he goes to work for a major manufacturer (IBM, Remington, Burroughs, Olivetti), he'll first learn repair of the basic typewriter styles and dictating equipment produced by that particular company. These companies prefer applicants who have had two years of college. If he does particularly well, he may receive further training on more sophisticated machines. The repairmen with the very best mechanical ability will be trained to repair composers, which themselves may be tied into computers.

Some of the best repairmen are lost to the career when they enter sales work for the manufacturer.

It is also relatively easy, from a capital investment point of view, to become self-employed. After several years of experience with repair shops, an individual can open his own business.

SOME FACTS

In 1974 about 65,000 office machine repairmen were employed in the United States. The U.S. Department of Labor predicts that the need for repairmen will increase rapidly, 3,000 newly trained technicians per year, through the 1980's. Parker estimates an even greater need of 10,000 qualified repairmen a year.

Office machine repairmen perform the routine maintenance on typewriters, adding machines and calculators, cash registers, dictating machines, postage meters, and duplicating and copying machines. When one of these pieces of equipment breaks down, the repairman must diagnose and correct the trouble.

Some repairmen sell office supplies—ink, paper, ribbons, stencils—as part of their work and may receive some commission on sales.

Tools involved in the trade include screwdrivers, pliers, and test equipment like meters and gauges.

Pay rates in 1974 ranged from $165 to $300 per week. Persons who can only repair typewriters are considered the least skilled members of the trade and receive a salary near the lower end of the range. Those who can repair accounting machines and complex duplicating machines are paid closer to the top of the scale.

Office machine repair is considered lighter, cleaner work than most skilled trades. Often employees work in business suits or sport coats. In many cases, the repairmen travel around the community to the offices where equipment is to be serviced.

Training courses are available at both vocational schools and through correspondence. Once employed in the industry, an employee can expect to receive training from the manufacturers of the office equipment.

CLASSROOM WORK

Where classes are offered in office machine repair, often at a publicly funded occupational center, the first class is usually repair of IBM's most popular typewriter models. The next class involves repair of the increasingly popular IBM Selectric machine.

Students are also expected to take classes in basic and digital electronics and learn the repair of electronic calculators.

A practical lab is generally required, where students learn how to solder, use test equipment, and diagnose troubles.

Where there are enough students to warrant a class, repair of Olivetti, Smith-Corona, and other typewriter makes is taught. Some schools also have teaching tapes, which allow a student to proceed at his own learning rate.

A working knowledge of at least general math is required in order to survive the classroom work.

RELATED CAREERS

Some of the most talented office machine repairmen become computer technicians, doing repairs on sophisticated equipment.

Other repairmen become full-time salesmen of office supplies and equipment.

Chapter XVI

Operating Engineers

Noah Belnavis carefully manipulates the pedal and hand controls of his crane to raise the huge cement slab and then lower it carefully into place. The job requires coordination, concentration, and alertness.

Across town on another construction job, Dave Gee works the controls of his backhoe to remove the dirt from a future apartment house basement garage. The backhoe rocks and bounces Dave as he drives across the uneven site.

Both Noah and Dave are apprentice operating engineers.

"Crane work is the lazy man's job," says Noah, age twenty-six. "It takes a lot more brain work and concentration than operating some of the other machines, but it's not so physically hard."

In the trade, the crane operator is recognized as the most skilled of all the occupations and is paid accordingly. Noah, now in his third and final year of apprentice training, is looking forward to a nearly $10-per-hour journeyman's rate in the Los Angeles area.

It's not surprising that Noah has found a niche for himself in the highest-skilled job. He is an ambitious, intelligent young man and works hard at it.

Noah moved from his Jamaica birthplace about seven years ago, seeking the better opportunities available in the United States. He attended college and has the degrees necessary to teach vocational education (auto mechanics) in the public schools.

"Jamaica is very poor," says Noah. "I thought I could better make something of myself if I came here. I somehow lost interest in auto mechanics, and now I'm making twice as much money as a crane operator as I would be as a teacher. But Jamaica is still home."

Noah and his Jamaica-born wife plan some day to go back to their homeland. With enough capital, Noah can become a contractor.

Once Noah applied to the operating engineers union for admission as an apprentice, he didn't have to wait long for an opening. He had scored exceptionally high on the entrance test. He has invested about $80 in hand tools, and his union dues are $13 per month.

"If you can get into a closed-shop union trade, it is a marvelous way to make something of yourself," says Noah.

Noah's classmate, Dave Gee, has been an apprentice for a little more than one year. So far, he has operated Caterpillars, trench diggers, graders, and his favorite, the backhoe.

"Sometimes, the boss seems to forget I'm just an apprentice and asks too much of me," says Dave. "He'll have me going down steep banks before I think I'm ready for it. If I get in trouble, I can jump off, of course, but I don't want to wreck the machine and lose my job, too."

Dave has yet to operate a conveyor, a task Noah finds among the most boring and tedious, even if it is easy physically.

Both Noah and Dave have worked steadily for their same respective contractors for over a year. A contractor has a choice of keeping good workers and laying off those who don't produce.

"They won't give it to you on a silver platter," says Dave. "You have to work at it."

Dave had graduated from high school early and was attending a community college when he had a chance to land a $6-per-hour construction laborer's job. The money looked good, so he took the job. Later, one of the journeymen operating engineers suggested that Dave take the apprenticeship test.

"The test was kind of hard," recalls Dave. "I hadn't done a fraction problem in years." It was nearly three years from the time Dave took the test until his name reached the top of the list.

"Working as a laborer, I thought machine operator looked like a pretty easy job," says Dave. "It is harder than I thought. It's mentally tiring; you really have to concentrate. And it's physically hard, too. Then you have to go to school two nights a week, and sometimes there is homework to do."

According to Dave's instructor, Bill Ungles, the work will get easier. With time and practice, the operation of the machine becomes second nature. The operator learns to sit back and let the machine do the work.

Ungles feels that the apprentices who will make the grade are those who are willing to put out 110 percent effort and learn more about their jobs than just the minimum requirements. Most apprentices don't have any real trouble with the classroom work, but some have trouble getting back into the habit of attending school regularly.

Once a month, night classes are canceled and the class meets for five hours on Saturday at the union-sponsored practice construction site. Here, the students have a chance to get hands-on experience with all of the various machines they will be required to operate when they are journeymen.

When a student enters the apprenticeship program, he can choose one of several courses of study. He may elect to be equipment operator, heavy-duty repairman, plant equipment operator, dredge operator, or rock, sand, and gravel expert. The apprentice has the option of changing specialty any time during the training period.

Most of the classes are taken by all of the apprentices, no matter which specialty. A mechanic, however, doesn't have to learn about grade checking, and an operator doesn't need as much information about the repair of engines.

Competition for the limited apprentice openings is keen.

In 1976 the Los Angeles local of the operating engineers union had 450 applicants for 32 openings. Of the total number of applicants, 47 were women; 2 were accepted. The union officials and night class instructors are very optimistic that these two young women will make the grade and are the forerunners of more females in the trade.

The qualifying test includes verbal ability, reading comprehension, math, and mechanical aptitude. Those who do not score high enough to be accepted may reapply the following year.

"If a kid does well in the industry," says Ungles, "he can choose all kinds of new directions. He can work his way up to foreman or superintendent, or he can work for the union as a coordinator of the joint apprenticeship committee or even business agent."

Ungles, in addition to his part-time teaching job, is an equipment salesman.

SOME FACTS

In 1974 there were 275,000 operating engineers in the United States, plus 125,000 bulldozer operators. It is expected that 18,500 new operators will have to be trained each year to meet the moderately growing demand for skilled personnel through the 1980's.

Operating engineers are at the controls of bulldozers, cranes, trench diggers, paving machines, derricks, hoists, air compressors, trench-pipe layers, and dredges.

The task requiring the highest skill level is that of operating a crane. The operator is required to manipulate a number of pedals and levers to rotate the crane and raise and lower its boom and load-line. He also manipulates the different kinds of equipment that can be attached to the crane booms, such as buckets for lifting dirt or wrecking balls for demolishing old buildings.

The operation of the earth-moving machines requires the least skill.

Operators may also make minor repairs on their equipment, but heavy-duty equipment mechanics make the major repairs. An operator may have to invest $80 to $90 in small hand tools to make the necessary repairs. A mechanic may own $1,000 worth of tools.

Most operating engineers work for contractors on highway, dam, mass-transit, airport, or other large-scale construction projects. Other operating engineers may be employed by utility companies or manufacturers who do their own construction work. State and local public works departments also employ operating engineers.

Because of the large capital investment required, few operating engineers become self-employed.

Often an apprentice's first tasks involve oiling, cleaning, greasing, repairing, and starting machines. Within a year, he is driving a machine that is worth a half million dollars.

In 1974 the average wage in the United States for crane operator was $8.40 per hour; bulldozer operator, $8.25; air compressor operator, $7.35. An apprentice typically starts at 70 percent of the local journeyman's rate and receives regular increases during his three years of training.

Because of the constant movement, shakes, and jolts of the equipment, the work is considered physically tiring, particularly the operation of bulldozers and scrapers. Kidney problems are not unusual among long-time operators, and they often wear a belt for support.

High-school students interested in this occupation should take classes in auto mechanics and basic math.

CLASSROOM WORK

During classroom time, apprentices receive an introduction to the construction industry, review safety procedures and the motor vehicle code, and learn Red Cross first-aid methods.

In other courses, students learn about moving earth, heavy

equipment repair, rock, sand, and gravel operations, dredging, and rock products.

Appropriate math is taught, as well as electrical theory (Delco), diesel, high compression and internal combustion engines.

Cable splicing, hydraulics, and welding are a part of the course.

Chapter XVII

Plumbers

The 170 employees at Advance Plumbing in Long Beach, California, specialize in large industrial jobs. They construct refineries, breweries, and steel plants. They have maintenance contracts with many of the plants they have helped to build. And they have the commercial contract for the plumbing in most of the Jack-in-the-Box restaurants across the country.

Patrick Mulvaney is proud to be one of the four apprentice plumbers working for Advance.

Pat has been an apprentice for only six months, and this is the second contractor for whom he has worked. He is following in the footsteps of his father and two uncles who have earned their livings as plumbers.

About two years ago, Pat completed his application for apprentice training with the union and took the test.

"I remember there was a lot of math on the test," recalls Pat. "Some of it was algebra, but most was basic arithmetic. There were some skill questions, like what is a wrench and what do you do with it. There were spatial relations questions and some drafting. And then to test our manual dexterity, we had to put pegs in the holes on a big board."

Pat was one of the 250 applicants who passed the test out of a total of 500 who took it. Then came the oral interview by the joint apprenticeship committee.

"They asked why I wanted to get into the trade," says Pat, "and what I expected to do with it in the future. They seemed really concerned that I didn't have an arrest record, particularly for alcohol or drugs. I understand they used to really rate a guy down if he had long hair, but I don't think they do that so much anymore."

There may also be questions about the applicant's attitude toward unions.

Fortunately, Pat was rated high by the interviewers. This particular local union employs about thirty new apprentices every two years, fewer if construction activity is slow. In spite of a high placement number, Pat had to wait for his chance for almost two years.

Affirmative action programs, the effort to enroll more minority racial groups and women in apprenticeship programs, affected Pat's standing on the eligibility list.

A representative of the joint apprenticeship committee recalls one Caucasian young man who was rated fifth on the list but was moved to twenty-third by the time the hiring list was brought into the racial balance requirements of the affirmative action program.

Pat's first assignment when he was sent out by the union hiring hall was to an apartment complex under construction.

"I ran errands, measured and cut pipe, dug ditches, and did clean-up work," recalls Pat. "The journeyman I was working with was really helpful and taught me a lot."

Now at Advance, Pat spends some time out on a job and the rest in the plumbing yard. At the yard, he restocks returned parts to the appropriate shelves, threads pipe, runs the forklift, and sometimes paints or does clean-up around the yard.

"I've really enjoyed all the work so far," says Pat. "I guess you have to like to work with your hands and not be afraid to get your hands dirty. You have to be patient, too. Some guys feel they know it all after a couple of months. They'll learn more if they listen and do what they're asked."

Pat thinks math, drafting, and shop classes are important for a future plumber to take in high school. He feels he could have benefited from some science classes that would have helped him understand mineral deposits in the water and different soil conditions.

Pat is obviously the kind of apprentice his boss, Jimmy Blanchard, likes to have around.

"I like to see boys who want to work and are willing to use their brain," says Blanchard. "Sometimes I have to send an ap-

Pat cuts pipe in the plumbing yard shop.

prentice back to the union hiring hall. If that happens, it's usually because he has no mechanical ability or is just not interested in the work."

Blanchard is also an evening instructor of apprenticeship classes. In order to qualify for that job, he had to take special training beyond his own journeyman's rating. He has spent five of his summer weeks at Purdue University qualifying himself in teaching methods, psychology, and motivation.

"If the kids have trouble in class it's usually because they don't know basic math," says Blanchard. "Some can't even figure percentages. Some don't write clearly enough so you can read it, either."

Blanchard certainly enjoys his work with the apprentices. He has even appeared in court to help get a student out of trouble.

Another apprentice, Patrick Flowers, works across town and has been in the trade for three years. He, like Pat Mulvaney, is following in his father's footsteps, and his mother is a secretary for the joint apprenticeship committee.

His connections didn't really help Patrick become an apprentice, however. He had to qualify on his own by taking the three- to four-hour entry test.

Patrick has been fortunate to work for the same contractor for the last two years and so has been unemployed very little.

"I like the job I'm on now," says Patrick. "I can stay on the same job long enough to do the groundwork for the new homes and then put in the fixtures."

Groundwork (installing the initial pipes) can be hot, sweaty, and physical, particularly in the summer.

"Like my dad told me," recalls Patrick, "the first two years are the lousiest, when you don't know anything. But if you stick it out, everything falls into place."

Patrick's mother watches over the apprentices at her local. Apprentices are not required to come into the hiring hall every day when they are out of work, though some of them do. Mrs. Flowers has been known to take home the list of out-of-work apprentices to call at night if she had trouble finding an eligible boy at home when there was a late afternoon request from an employer.

"The kids really need the work, so I do what I can to help them," says Mrs. Flowers. "They aren't supposed to hustle their own job, though sometimes the union looks the other way if times are hard."

Currently, this local is running 50 percent unemployment of their apprentices.

"We don't have a very high dropout rate for apprentices," says Mrs. Flowers. "When we do expel someone, it's because they aren't paying their dues or they have not been attending the classes."

Getting hired as an apprentice in a nonunion shop works rather differently. These small shops do primarily home repair and maintenance jobs. They typically have few employees and one or two helpers or apprentices.

Ralph Anderson, a boss/owner of a small shop says, "When I'm looking for a new employee, I like to feel him out to see if he really enjoys mechanical work. I want him to be the kind of person who can make decisions by himself, since someday he'll be out on a job alone. I want to know he can add and subtract, and I want to be able to read his handwriting. A customer isn't too happy if he gets a bill for $200 and can't figure out what it's for."

This employer looks for applicants who don't change jobs too frequently. He would rather hire someone who has been a box boy for two years with the same grocery store than someone who has worked two weeks each for six different plumbers.

Anderson is impressed with applicants who reapply even though he didn't have an opening for them the first time.

"I like high-school graduates," he says, "because that means they can stick to something. And I don't want them to have any of their own problems, like no transportation."

Appearance is important in the plumbers Anderson hires. They meet the public, often housewives, and must make a favorable impression.

Anderson gives a new employee a trial period. He sends the apprentice out on the job with different journeymen each day to test the young person's ability and interest. And Anderson may take him on a job himself.

A few women are finding success and acceptance as apprentice plumbers. For women with adequate strength, mechanical ability, and interest, the unionized plumbing apprentice programs offer an excellent opportunity for training. In most cases, local unions have not been able to satisfy affirmative action quotas for females. If a woman can pass the qualifying test, she would no doubt rank high on the placement list. Because all apprentices are referred from the union hiring hall, unlike carpenter apprentices who have to hustle their own jobs, a female should find only minimum resistance from employers, assuming she is prepared for the physical nature of the work.

Members of other minority groups will also find good acceptance in the trade.

SOME FACTS

In 1974 some 375,000 plumbers and pipefitters were employed in the United States, compared to over a million carpenters. The demand for plumbers is expected to increase moderately through the 1980's, with a need for 16,300 new plumbers to be trained each year.

At least part of the increased demand for plumbers is because of the trend in new home construction to provide more bathrooms, air conditioners, washing machines, and kitchen waste disposal units.

The largest demand will be in those areas where new construction is occurring. That means that metropolitan areas will have few openings for apprentices, but sprawling suburbs will provide greater opportunities. Since an apprentice is allowed to change local unions only once during his training, it is advisable to pick a fast-growing area for application for entry into the occupation.

Although plumbers and pipefitters are often thought of as having the same occupation, their work is different.

A plumber installs water, gas, and waste disposal systems in homes, schools, factories, and other buildings. They "rough in" (install) pipe systems during the early phases of construction, and in the final phases they install heating and air-conditioning units, water heaters, and fixtures (sinks, tubs, etc.).

Pipefitters, rather than constructing homes and buildings, work more typically in heavy industry. They install high- and low-pressure pipes that carry hot water, steam, liquids, and gases, often in oil refineries, the chemical industry, or food-processing plants.

A plumber must know how to use the following hand tools: wrenches, reamers, drills, braces and bits, hammers, chisels, and saws. Power machines may be used to cut, bend, and thread pipe. Plumbers may also use gas or acetylene torches, and welding, soldering, and brazing equipment.

Most plumbers work for plumbing contractors in the new construction business. A substantial number, however, are self-employed or work for contractors doing repair and modernization of existing homes and buildings.

Some plumbers work for government agencies or public utilities. Others are involved in maintenance of industrial and commercial buildings.

Apprentice plumbers start at 40 to 50 percent of the journeyman's wage rate and receive a 5 percent raise every six months.

In 1974 the average pay in the United States for journeyman plumbers was close to $9.00 per hour. This rate is above the average of all building-trades journeymen.

Generally, plumbers are affected less by seasonal factors than are carpenters.

CLASSROOM WORK

Apprentice plumbers are required to attend school two nights a week during their five years of training. The classes may be conducted by the union at a union facility, or the students may attend a local public trade school.

Occasionally, when unemployment rates are high, there may

be cutbacks in the classes offered, and apprentices have to attend classes only one night per week.

Students learn mathematics for plumbing and pipefitting, elementary drawing and layout, and principles of water supply and distribution. They become familiar with charts and conversion tables, metric systems, structural standards of fixture design and their uses.

Water pollution, bacteriological problems, and backflow prevention are studied in the third year of training.

Some algebra, geometry, and trigonometry are involved when learning the skill.

In the final year of training, the student learns local and national building codes and how to establish himself as a plumbing contractor.

Early in the training, there are discussions of the role of unions in labor relations, presumably presented with a slant favoring the activities of the plumber's union and the importance of following the rules established by the union.

Chapter XVIII

Printers

Think of the sound your car windshield wipers make. Then multiply that sound by a hundred and you'll hear the rhythmic beat of a printing press. Multiply again times the number of printing presses at work and you'll hear the beat of a roomful of presses thumping against reams of paper, one page at a time.

The noise is not overpowering—certainly not as loud as a drag strip on a Sunday afternoon—but you must raise your voice to be heard and understood.

At Dunn Brothers Printing, thirty employees work in a room half the size of a football field. Most are gray-haired men with years of experience in the trade. In the binding department, four women put the finishing touches on commercial printing jobs. And there are three apprentices at work—young men aged eighteen to twenty-two.

Almost surprisingly, none of the employees have ink-stained hands or wear protective clothing. A handy bottle of bleach keeps hands looking as trim as any white-collar worker's. Standard work clothes seem to survive an occasional spill of ink.

Glenn Sarpy is the least experienced of the three apprentices at this middle-sized printing firm.

"My uncle is a foreman here," explains Glenn. "We had talked about my coming into the printing business for a long time, and when I graduated from high school it seemed like the right thing to do."

During his nine months as an apprentice letterpress operator,

Glenn has learned to run two machines—a windmill type and a vertical or cylinder type. Under the supervision of a journeyman letterpress operator, Glenn fills the machine with ink and paper, starts and stops the machinery, and has the dirty task of washing down the machine when the run is completed.

This particular print shop has one larger horizontal machine

Glenn is learning to operate a letterpress.

that Glenn will learn to operate as he becomes more experienced.

"They say letterpress is a dying craft," says Glenn, "but I should be able to transfer over to offset printing pretty easily, and then I'll be able to get a job anywhere."

Glenn doesn't think of himself as an expert yet, even on the machines he has learned to operate.

"There's a lot to learn about inks and paper and which ink to use on which paper," says Glenn. He doesn't expect to be bored during his four years of apprenticeship training.

Although the formal apprenticeship agreement requires Glenn to attend school 144 hours a year in addition to his working hours, Glenn hasn't begun any classes yet. He plans to begin a night class soon at Los Angeles Trade Technical College, a public school about ten miles from his home.

Glenn considers himself lucky, at age eighteen, to have a well-paying, steady job in the printing industry.

"I think a kid ought to look beyond just the beginning pay," says Glenn. "The printing business will always be around. We don't have the ups and downs of aerospace. And I'm not out of a job if it rains. With the union I've got really good benefits like medical insurance."

Glenn's union dues are $18 per month. Every time a member of the union dies, the remaining members are assessed one dollar as a contribution to the widow and children of the deceased member. Glenn also tries to attend the monthly meetings of his union. He was required to pay an $83 initiation fee to the union out of his first month's income.

Craig Ramsey is in his third year of a four-year apprenticeship program learning offset printing, the highest-paid job for craftsmen in the industry.

A thoughtful twenty-two-year-old, Craig likes the standard 35-hour workweek in the industry that allows him free time to pursue his other interests, which include hunting, fishing, and learning sign language so that he can work with deaf children.

Craig began work with Dunn Brothers on a part-time basis while he was still in high school. He landed the part-time job in the binding department based on the recommendation of a high-school printing teacher who is a personal friend of one of the Dunn brothers.

Craig continued on a part-time basis while he attended two years of junior college, majoring in printing. During that time, he was awarded a scholarship from the publishing firm William C. Brown.

After graduation, Craig was faced with a decision. Should he continue his education at a four-year school majoring in printing management or work toward a journeyman's rating as an offset printer? Based at least in part on the need for income and the lack of a guaranteed job if he did get a degree, Craig went to work as an apprentice.

Craig, an apprentice offset printer, likes the standard 35-hour workweek in the industry.

"The interesting part of the job is setting it up," says Craig as he points out the row of ink control keys on the two-color press. "You need to set the ink flow just right depending on whether it's just typed copy or a solid, filled-in picture you're printing. After you get the run set up, then you just watch the machine work. Sometimes it takes three days to run one job, and that can get a little monotonous."

The large Heidelberg press Craig operates requires two men and a constant flow of paper.

As Craig lifts forty to fifty pounds of thirty-six inch paper into the machine for the third time in fifteen minutes, he says, "An apprentice usually gets stuck doing the dirty work the journeyman doesn't want to do."

Craig thinks an apprentice should make an effort to operate all the machines he can and learn as much as possible about inks, paper, and other processes, like stripping. "That broadens your perspective of the job and makes it more interesting," says Craig.

Jerry Collins has a brand-new ticket to prove to the world that he is a journeyman graphic arts finisher. And he couldn't be more proud of his job or more pleased with his future as a craftsman.

Jerry has been training for the printing business since junior high school, when he took print shop as an elective. At his high-school graduation, he received the award for outstanding industrial arts student.

"Usually that award went to a woodworking student who had made a desk for the teacher," Jerry says with considerable pride. "I was the first printing student ever to get the award."

After graduation, Jerry worked for a year in a nonunion print shop as a pressman on vertical presses. "That work was a little dirty," recalls Jerry. "It's much cleaner here in the bindery department. My sister was working here at Dunn Brothers, and she helped me get this job."

Jerry works on machines that cut, stitch, fold, and gather the paper. After he finishes with his work, the job is ready to be shipped to the customer.

Jerry's apprenticeship was a full five years, although he earned the journeyman's wage rate for about a year before the apprenticeship committee gave its final approval.

During the first three years of apprenticeship, Jerry attended trade school one night a week.

"I was really discouraged at first," recalls Jerry. "I was nearly a full-time cutter here at the plant, and at school the teacher kept asking me to show the other kids how to run the cutter. I had to insist that I get a chance to learn the other machines."

After three years of trade school, Jerry had taken all of the available finishing classes, so the apprenticeship requirement for continued classes was waived.

Jerry lifts two to three tons of paper a day as a graphic arts finisher.

Outside of the printing classes Jerry took in high school, he thinks the most valuable class he took was physical education. He continues a physical fitness program by lifting weights.

"I lift two to three tons of paper a day," says Jerry, "and you really have to have a strong back for that."

Jerry is likely to work for Dunn Brothers a long time. He considered applying for a civil service job a year ago but found it paid $300 less per month than his current union wage rate.

Jerry, his wife, and two young sons moved into their own

home recently. He uses some of his four weeks a year of vacation time, after five years of employment, to turn their house into a home.

Someday Jerry may become a foreman, which will raise his pay by about $10 a week but will mean less physical labor for him.

Glenn, Craig, and Jerry are typical of the apprentices Stan Dunn likes to hire. They have the three qualities he looks for in his young employees: strength, manual dexterity, and mental alertness.

"Most of these fellows will move 300 to 400 pounds of paper an hour," says Dunn. "I want to be sure I hire young men who are physically developed enough to do the job."

"When I interview a youngster, I want to know that he likes to work with his hands. Maybe he works on his car or fixes clocks in his spare time. I don't much care what he has done with his hands, but there has to be some evidence that he really enjoys it."

"I've never asked about high-school grades, and I really prefer junior college graduates, but any applicant has to impress me as being mentally alert. These boys work on equipment that is worth $100,000 and they run $250 worth of paper through a machine in an hour. If they mess up for just ten minutes, it can ruin $50 to $75 worth of paper. And some of the machinery, like the cutter, can be very dangerous. I don't want any of these boys to lose a hand because they were careless."

For specific jobs, Dunn may look for special abilities. "A Linotype operator needs to know spelling and punctuation. A compositor should be comfortable with simple math problems. A paper cutter has to handle fractions quickly," he says. "I've found, though, that once an employee starts working with fractions, he catches on fast even if he was never good in math in high school."

Dunn Brothers has never had an apprentice drop out of its program. Dunn hires apprentices only when he knows he will have a job for them when they get their journeyman ticket, a policy not followed by all print shops.

"A journeyman would be capable of starting his own printing business, but it would cost easily $50,000 just for the equipment," says Dunn. "Most of our employees stay with us a long time."

"We never have many openings for apprentices; in fact, we usually only have one on the payroll at a time. Right now, we are planning ahead for the retirement of several of our workers, so we have to train their replacements."

Union agreements restrict the number of allowable apprentices in relation to the number of journeymen employed, and an apprentice must always work with a journeyman.

"Since we have so few openings, we almost always hire based on the recommendation of a friend or relative who is an employee or in the trade," says Dunn. "I think that's pretty typical of the industry. There's a lot of nepotism."

Employer policies can vary widely. To become an offset lithograph pressman apprentice at American Can Company, not far from Dunn Brothers, the procedure is quite different.

This can-manufacturing plant employs 400 people. The apprentice jobs are considered a promotion for the semiskilled employees. Longtime employees, often with fifteen years or more with the company, are the ones who get the opportunity to learn a craft. Although seniority is the only factor in selection, the department supervisor looks for the same qualities in his employees as does Dunn—energy, common sense, alertness, and a willingness to learn and try hard.

There are two striking differences between being a printer at Dunn Brothers and American Can. At American Can, the printers are decorating metal, rather than paper, and it is extremely noisy.

"Working on metal creates some problems in getting just the

right balance between ink and water in the printing mixture," says the department supervisor. "It's so different from working on absorbent paper that our printers would have to be retrained if they wanted to change jobs to a paper printing outfit. What they learn in regular printing schools is helpful here, but we are very specialized."

Toy manufacturers are one of the few other employers who do metal decorating.

The program is so specialized that often regular apprentice classes are not available. The company sends the apprentice to special classes on ink or machinery operation as they become available, often from the manufacturer of the product.

During the course of their four-year apprenticeship, the American Can lithographers must learn about the setting and operation of Magnetic and Dexter Feed machines, side gauges and pusher fingers, grippers, trip fingers, cylinders, ink rollers, dampening systems, solutions, printing plates, inks, ovens (for drying finished sheets of tin) and clean-up of the presses and rollers.

The machinery is as large as the printing presses at a newspaper. It is so noisy in the printing room, and throughout the manufacturing plant, that earplugs must be worn. Conversation, except in the office areas, is difficult.

SOME FACTS

In 1970 there were about 13,800 registered apprentices in the printing industry. Although that number has remained relatively constant over the years, growth is expected in the industry through the 1980's, as printers keep up with the increasing demands for the printed page.

The increased use of computers and cold printing processes make the printing industry a changing one. Mechanization has reduced the number of positions requiring hand skills, such as bindery finishers.

Half of the nation's printers are employed in the metropolitan areas of New York, Illinois, California, Pennsylvania, and Ohio. Outside of those areas, most printing employees work in the newspaper industry rather than with commercial or job printing establishments.

Each commercial establishment tends to specialize in a certain type of printing. For instance, Dunn Brothers specializes in printing forms and contracts for the insurance industry.

Occupational specialties in the printing industry include composition, platemaking, press work, and binding. Journeyman pay rates in 1975 in the Los Angeles area ranged from $4.80 per hour for bindery finishers to $8.78 per hour for printing pressman.

Most apprentices start at 60 percent of the journeyman wage rate, with 5 percent pay increases every six months until they complete the four- to five-year apprenticeship (two years for bindery finishers). Union contracts usually provide for time-and-a-half pay for hours worked over 35 per week, the standard workweek in the industry, as well as medical, vacation, and retirement fringe benefits.

Nonunion shops do not have formal apprenticeship programs leading to a journeyman ticket, and the wages and fringe benefits vary considerably from one shop to another.

High-school print shop classes provide a useful background for entry-level jobs. Other classes that are of value in some printing occupations include art, drafting, mechanical drawing, chemistry, photography, English, spelling, typing, electronics, and journalism.

In general, printing occupations require good eyesight, average physical strength, manual dexterity, mental alertness, and normal color vision.

Women are finding some acceptance in printing occupations where heavy lifting is not required. Newspapers may employ women in graphic arts and cold process lithographic jobs, including camera work, stripping, and platemaking.

CLASSROOM WORK

The formal apprenticeship agreements in the printing industry require the apprentice to complete 144 hours of classroom learning per year, in addition to his regular work shift.

In reality, the classroom hours seem to be more flexible than is suggested by the written agreement. New apprentices do not necessarily begin taking classes immediately. And experienced apprentices may complete all available courses before they have served the full term of their apprenticeship.

It is clear, however, that during the major portion of the term of apprenticeship, classes must be taken. In a metropolitan area, the classes are available at a public trade school. Most apprentices attend classes one or two evenings per week. They are not paid for this classroom time.

Course content varies slightly, but the following suggests a general description of courses available in the various printing specialties:

Bindery Courses. Theory and operation of folding machines, paper cutters, stitching machines, drilling and punching machines, perforators, table work activities, sewing machines, and automatic collating machines. Bookbinding, stock identification and estimating, and pamphlet binding are also offered.

Graphic Arts Courses. Typography, composition, composing room machinery operation and maintenance, imposition and lockup, printer's math, proofreading, cost and estimating of jobs, cold type composition, and printing papers and ink.

Letterpress Courses. Operation of vertical, cylinder, and flatbed presses, color imprinting, and inks.

Offset Presswork Courses. Theory and operation of offset presses of various sizes, including maintenance and use of color.

Photo-Offset Courses. Chemistry, physics, and mathematics of lithography, camera operation, halftone photography, color separation and corrections, stripping, etching, layout, and platemaking.

Chapter XIX

Tool and Diemakers

Barry Woodard and Bill Salfity machine titanium parts for jet engines. They work as apprentice tool and diemakers for a firm, Fansteel, whose products have helped put men on the moon.

"I had been working in a lot of job shops, but I wasn't getting anywhere," says Barry of his work experience before he got into the apprenticeship program. "At the job shops, I'd always have to start as a trainee. I wasn't learning to do the setups, just operate the machine."

The state employment office suggested to Barry that he apply for an industry-sponsored pre-apprenticeship class. To gain entry to the program, Barry had to take an aptitude test.

"The test wasn't too hard," recalls Barry. "There were some basic math questions and reading. Then we had to put pegs in holes on a board as fast as we could."

Barry became one of about twenty students in the twelve-week program. There are no guarantees of a job after completion of the program, but because it is sponsored by the National Tool and Die and Precision Machining Association,* the industry looks to the training classes for well-prepared entry-level employees.

"About half of our students stick with the program until graduation," says George Samoorian, instructor of the classes.

* For information about industry pre-apprenticeship training programs in your area, write to National Tool and Die and Precision Machining Association, 9300 Livingston Road, Washington, D.C. 20022.

"This year, all of our graduates went right to work, and we actually had other requests we couldn't fill. We make a special effort to enroll men of minority racial backgrounds and women. So far, we've had three women graduates and they're all doing well."

During the five-day-a-week, seven-hour-a-day classes, Barry

Barry got his start in an industry-sponsored pre-apprenticeship program.

learned shop terminology, the parts of the machine, safety procedures, shop math, including algebra, and how to run a lathe, drill press, mill, and grinder. He was paid $50 a week while in school, about the amount he would have drawn on unemployment benefits.

Barry was referred to Fansteel for an interview when he completed the pretraining. The personnel manager interviewed him.

"Mostly, he just wanted to know how much I wanted to be a

tool and die maker," says Barry. "I think they wanted to be sure I'd stick with it."

Barry's schooling continues, since he has to attend apprenticeship classes one night a week during the four-year program. During this first six months, the emphasis is on geometry. Fortunately, a high-school class in drafting has helped Barry understand the current geometry.

Although Barry doesn't like to get his hands dirty on the job, which often happens, he does find the work challenging.

"I like to work to close tolerances," says Barry. "I like to machine something and have it come out perfect." He likes new assignments that give him a chance to try new skills.

"I don't know why anybody would drop out of an apprentice program," says Barry. "You're on the job earning a living and going to school, too. It's better than college. It would have taken me ten years of experience in job shops to get this kind of experience."

Bill used a different route to enter the apprentice program. He attended a regional occupational school four hours a day during his junior and senior years in high school. It was the teacher at the occupational center who recommended Bill for the job at Fansteel.

Like Barry, Bill likes jobs in which he is learning new skills. "Sometimes, we have to run the same part through the machine over and over," says Bill. "That can get boring."

Bill took algebra in high school but didn't have any interest at the time, so didn't do well. Now he is taking algebra at a community college night class. He also attends the one-night-a-week class for apprentices.

"We've learned basic tools, safety practices, and shop theory," says Bill. "The only time I have trouble is when the class is doing something more advanced than I have done at work, like heat treatment. Then I have to ask the older guys at work to explain the stuff to me."

Bill has been an apprentice about one and a half years. In that time, he has invested a little over $200 in his own hand tools.

"Attitude is the most important thing on this job," according to Bill. "You have to be able to follow instructions and use your head at the same time."

Bill machines titanium parts on a vertical lathe.

Burt Richardson, personnel director for Fansteel and chairman of the industry apprenticeship committee, explains the difference between training to be a tool and die maker or a machinist.

"Tool and die, jig and fixture, general machinist, and mold maker are all apprenticeable trades," says Richardson. "During the first two years of apprenticeship, they all learn pretty much the same thing. The emphasis is on machining. The machinists will go on to learn complex setups that involve compound angles.

They increase the speed of machining and work with different metals.

"The tool and die makers will get more involved in grinding and filing operations to very close tolerances. They'll learn to make a die, which may be in several parts. Then the die is put in a punch press and metal is formed to make a part for some other machine."

When Richardson hires a new apprentice, he is primarily concerned about attitude.

"I want to be sure the man wants to stick in this as a career," he says. "I check with his teacher about attendance, attitude, the quality of his machining projects, and if he can follow instructions. The foreman looks for the eager-beaver type who wants to learn."

In addition to hiring new apprentices out of occupational schools or the pre-apprenticeship training, Fansteel has promoted its own employees into the position.

"Sometimes, we have a shop helper who has been doing a good job and seems well motivated," says Richardson. "We'll give him a chance on the machines."

Richardson feels that resistance to women in the trade is still strong but will probably decrease. "We're trying to get women into machining and welding, but there just aren't many women who are all that interested," he says.

SOME FACTS

In 1974 about 170,000 tool and die makers were employed in the United States, most of them in plants that manufacture machinery. Many work in Detroit, Flint, Chicago, and Los Angeles in the auto industry or aerospace.

A tool and die maker may produce jigs and fixtures, devices that hold metal while it is shaved, stamped, or drilled. They make gauges and other measuring devices for precision metal parts.

Diemakers construct metal forms (dies) to shape metal in

stamping and forging operations, which may include molding plastics. They also repair damaged jigs, fixtures, and dies.

Tool and die makers have a broad knowledge of machining operations, math, and blueprint reading. They must know the machining properties of various metals and alloys.

Tool and die makers learn to operate drill presses, milling machines, lathes, and grinders.

Demand for tool and die makers is expected to increase moderately through the 1980's. The growth of the trade may be limited by the increased use of numerically controlled machines that require less skill to operate.

(See Chapter XIII, "Machinists.")

Chapter XX

Some Other Apprenticeable Trades

Many of the jobs listed below are related to the construction industry. Keep in mind that although the hourly pay rates seem quite high, these jobs are often seasonal, and the demand for construction workers fluctuates from year to year. Periods of unemployment can be expected.

ASBESTOS WORKERS

Asbestos workers cover pipes, boilers, furnaces, and other equipment with asbestos or similar insulating material. The object of the job is to keep either hot or cold in or out. For instance, there is insulation material around heating ducts to prevent the heat from escaping before its intended destination.

The asbestos worker may install the material by pasting, wiring, taping, stud-welding, spraying, or plastering. Asbestos cement, tar paper, felt and plastic insulating material may be used.

In 1974 about 30,000 asbestos workers were employed in the United States, most of them by insulation contractors. Chemical plants, petroleum refineries, rubber plants, atomic energy installations, shipyards, and other industrial establishments that have extensive steam installations for power and heating are also frequent employers.

Although some asbestos workers are trained on the job as

helpers, some apprenticeship programs are available that provide general, all-around training.

The apprenticeship program is four years and includes night school instruction once or twice a week. Apprentices start at 50 to 60 percent of the journeyman's pay rate and receive increases every six months. In 1974 the average wage for asbestos workers in metropolitan areas was $9.35 per hour.

Applicants for apprentice positions must be high-school graduates or have passed the GED test. They are encouraged to have a background in English, shop math, blueprint reading, and metal shop. Since asbestos workers are often assigned work many miles from home, a driver's license and a reliable car are important.

Employment prospects through the 1980's appear good for asbestos workers. The demand for insulation as a way to save fuel and energy will help keep the demand for asbestos workers somewhat higher than for other construction workers.

Working with asbestos presents some health hazards. At the very least, many people, particularly those with fair skin, are allergic to asbestos and contract a skin rash.

BOILERMAKERS

Boilermaking is heavy, often hazardous, metal work.

Boilermakers fabricate and assemble boilers, tanks, vats, and other containers of heavy steel plates. The boilers supply steam that drives the huge turbines in electric utility plants and on ships. The tanks and vats may be used to process and store chemicals or oil. Boilermakers also work in new ship construction and repair damaged hulls, bulkheads, and deck plates by removing the old plates and installing new ones.

A boilermaker, working from blueprints, lays out the work, cuts to size and shape, drills, punches, bends, welds, bolts, and rivets as necessary.

In 1974 about 45,000 boilermakers were employed in the

United States. Most worked in the construction industry, but iron and steel plants, petroleum refineries, railroads, shipyards, and electric power plants are also frequent employers. The federal government, particularly at shipyards and power plants, also employs boilermakers.

Apprenticeship training is the best way to learn the trade. The training program is three to four years and includes evening classes. Apprentices generally start at 70 to 75 percent of the journeyman's pay rate. Pay rates for journeymen vary rather widely, depending upon whether the boilermaker is working in field erection or in a shop. Field work is more hazardous and is generally considered more difficult, and therefore the pay rates are higher, averaging $8.60 per hour in 1974. In a shop, a journeyman is more likely to earn in the area of $5.50 an hour but is subject to fewer periods of unemployment.

Employment prospects look good through the 1980's. This will be particularly true if there is a great increase in the number of nuclear power plants or other power generators built during that period.

Young people interested in careers as boilermakers are encouraged to take classes in mechanical drawing, blueprint reading, metal shop, basic mathematics, and welding.

BRICKLAYERS

To no one's surprise, bricklayers lay brick. They may also lay concrete blocks, structural tile, or terra cotta. Stonemasonry is a related job that involves working with natural or artificial stone, usually on the exterior of buildings.

Bricklayers use chisels, trowels, jointers, tuck pointers, bricklayer's hammers, gauge lines, plumb bobs, and mason's levels. Power saws are often used for cutting and fitting bricks and other masonry materials.

In 1974 about 165,000 bricklayers and stonemasons were employed in the United States, almost all of them in the construction industry.

The apprenticeship program for bricklayers is three years. Like most apprentice programs, classroom work is required. Apprentices start at 50 percent of the journeyman's pay rate, which averaged $8.97 per hour in 1974.

The demand for new bricklayers is related to the general rise and fall of the construction business. The use of brick for decorative purposes and load-bearing walls continues to be popular and should keep employment prospects at least at an average level.

Young people interested in the trade are encouraged to take vocational courses including mechanical drawing, mathematics, blueprint reading, and shop classes.

CEMENT MASONS

The completion of a small patio or a huge dam both require the skills of a cement mason.

Cement masons finish the concrete surface on many types of construction projects. They may add color to the cement or special chemical additives that speed or slow the setting time. Because of the effects of heat, cold, and wind on the curing of cement, masons must be able to recognize by sight and touch what is occurring in the cement mixture so that they can prevent structural defects.

A cement mason uses special tools, such as a float, whip, or darby, to fill minor depressions and remove high spots. Hand- or power-operated trowels are used.

In 1974 about 90,000 cement masons were employed in the United States, most working for general contractors in the construction industry. A small number work for municipal public works departments, public utilities, and manufacturing firms that do their own construction work.

Apprenticeship training may be either a two-year or three-year program. In the classroom, apprentices learn applied mathematics, blueprint reading, and safety. Those involved in a three-year program also learn layout work and estimating.

Employment prospects for cement masons look good through the 1980's, as more homes, apartments, offices, and factories are built to meet the needs of our growing population.

Starting pay rates for apprentices vary between 50 percent and 75 percent of the journeyman's rate, which averaged $8.05 per hour in 1974.

Those interested in the career are encouraged to take classes in mechanical drawing, architectural drafting, shop courses, and mathematics.

GLAZIERS

A glazier works with a rather wide variety of glass products. He may install plate or window glass, structural glass, tempered and laminated glass, automobile windshields, or artistic glass in churches or other buildings. Plastics and porcelain materials may also be used.

Glaziers use hand tools such as glass cutters, putty knives, hack saws, drills, chisels, hammers, and screwdrivers. Occasionally, power cutting tools may be used.

About 36,000 glaziers were employed in the United States in 1974, about 9,000 of them in the construction industry. The rest were employed in factories, furniture manufacturing firms, or automotive repair. Demand for glaziers is expected to remain low. Only 700 newly trained glaziers will be needed nationwide each year through the 1980's.

The apprenticeship program is four years. Apprentices are paid 50 to 55 percent of the journeyman's rate, which in 1974 averaged $8.05 per hour. Many apprentices have first been helpers before entering the program.

Mathematics, art, mechanical drawing, and general shop classes are recommended for those interested in this career field.

IRONWORKERS

There is more than one kind of ironworker. Most of the movies about the giants of the construction industry have focused on the *structural ironworkers*. These men erect the steel framework of bridges, buildings, and large metal storage tanks. They also install steel floor decking in buildings and vault doors and their frames. Much of their work is done at great heights on narrow footings.

Reinforcing ironworkers may also work at great heights. Their job is to set steel bars into concrete forms to reinforce concrete structures.

An *ornamental ironworker* is more likely to have secure footing for his work. He installs metal stairways, catwalks, floor grating, and iron ladders or decorative ironwork on balconies, lamp-posts, gates, and fences.

Securely on the ground, the *shop ironworker* prefabricates iron and steel products for installation at the job site. He makes the steel beams, girders, and reinforcing sections that form the skeletons of skyscrapers, support highway overpasses, and constitute bridge spans.

All ironworkers use tools such as spud wrenches, hammers, burning and cutting torches, welding stingers, tapes, air guns, wrenches, pliers, levels, drills, and braces. Some employers require workers to furnish their own tools.

The term of apprenticeship training varies depending upon the type of ironwork involved. In the Los Angeles area, the number of years of apprenticeship is as follows:

Structural ironworker—3 years
Reinforcing ironworker—2 years

Ornamental ironworker—3 years
Shop ironworker—4 years

Apprentices start at 70 to 75 percent of the journeyman's rate of pay, which in 1974 averaged $8.65 per hour.

Young people interested in the trade are encouraged to take classes in mathematics, mechanical drawing, drafting, blueprint reading, metal shop, forge shop, and welding.

Employment prospects for ironworkers appear good through the 1980's.

LATHERS

Lathers install the backing that supports the plaster applied on walls and ceilings. This backing consists of metal lath, wire mesh, and gypsum board.

Depending upon the local union, apprenticeship programs may be two, three, or four years.

Applicants for apprenticeship programs may be as young as sixteen, which is lower than the usual minimum age in construction trades. However, high-school graduation is also required.

Apprentices start at 50 percent of the journeyman's pay rate, which in 1974 averaged $8.60 per hour.

Wood shop, welding, mathematics, blueprint reading, and mechanical drawing are suggested courses for future lathers.

The use of drywall materials in place of plaster has reduced the demand for lathers in recent years. There will continue to be a relatively small number of openings due to the need to replace lathers who retire, die, or transfer to other occupations.

PAINTERS AND PAPERHANGERS

Painting and paperhanging are separate trades, but many workers have learned the necessary skills for both types of work.

Painters apply paint, varnish, and other finishes to building surfaces to decorate or protect them. Paperhangers cover walls and ceilings of rooms with decorative wallpaper, fabric, vinyl, or similar materials.

Both painters and paperhangers must prepare the surface that is to be painted or covered. This may include some minor plaster patching, removal of old paper, and hole filling.

About 450,000 painters and 20,000 paperhangers were employed in 1974 in the United States, but little growth is expected in this trade through the 1980's. Job opportunities will be primarily due to experienced workers retiring or leaving the trade for other reasons.

Apprenticeship training is generally three years. Pay rates begin at 50 percent of the journeyman's wage, which in 1974 was $8.10 per hour. A rather high percentage of painters and paperhangers are self-employed.

Courses in art, chemistry, and wood shop are helpful to future painters. Ability to discern color is important.

PLASTERERS

Plasterers finish interior walls and ceilings with plaster coatings that form fire-resistant and relatively soundproof surfaces; they apply durable cement plaster or stucco to exterior surfaces. Some plasterers also cast ornamental designs in plaster.

In 1974 about 26,000 plasterers were employed in the United States, and it is estimated only 900 new apprentices nationwide need to be trained each year to keep up with demand.

Apprentices in the Los Angeles area, rather than attending night classes, attend school twice a year for nine consecutive working days. They are reimbursed for the time they spend in these classes.

Apprentices start at 50 percent of the journeyman's pay rate, which averaged $8.10 per hour in 1974.

Future plasterers are encouraged to take classes in mathematics, wood shop, blueprint reading, mechanical drawing, and art.

REFRIGERATION AND AIR-CONDITIONING MECHANICS

Refrigeration and air-conditioning mechanics install and repair equipment ranging in size from small window units to large central air-conditioning or refrigeration systems. When installing new equipment, they put the motors, compressors, evaporators, and other components in place, following blueprints and design specifications.

Generally, the employment is more steady for these skills than for others in construction-related trades. Often contractors install new equipment and then must maintain it over the years. Employers make an effort to maintain a permanent work crew, avoiding seasonal layoffs where possible.

Although it is possible to become a mechanic with only on-the-job training, apprenticeship programs are available in some areas. The training may be as long as five years.

Since this trade is not highly unionized, pay rates for journeymen vary widely, from $4.50 to $9.00 an hour in 1974.

Employment prospects appear good through the 1980's. Air conditioning in schools, factories, and other buildings, as well as homes, is expected to increase. The need for refrigeration equipment in the production, storage, and marketing of food products is expected to increase, too.

Helpful high-school courses include mathematics (through geometry), electric shop, machine shop, mechanical drawing, drafting, blueprint reading, and physics.

ROOFERS

Roofing can be a hot job. Contrary to popular opinion, people don't wait until the first rains to have the roof repaired. The roofer's busiest season is in the summer (particularly for new construction), which puts the worker on the roof, with no shade, standing next to his kettle of hot tar.

Roofers apply composition roofing and other materials, such as metal and tile, to the roofs of buildings. They also waterproof and dampproof walls and other building surfaces.

Although the majority of roofers learn their trade as helpers on the job, a three-year apprenticeship program is recommended.

Applicants for apprentice positions should have a background in mathematics through algebra, mechanical drawing, and blueprint reading. Apprentices start at 65 percent of the journeyman's rate, which in 1974 averaged $8.10 per hour.

Employment prospects for roofers appear good through the 1980's, with dampproofing and waterproofing becoming an increasingly important part of the work.

SHEET METAL WORKERS

Sheet metal work is one of the higher-paid skills in the construction industry. In 1974 the average pay for journeymen was $9.95 per hour.

These workers fabricate and install ducts for ventilating, air-conditioning, and heating systems. They also fabricate and install many other sheet metal products such as roofing, siding, and neon signs.

In addition to those employed in construction, other sheet metal workers are employed in the railroad, aircraft, and shipbuilding industries or in small shops that manufacture specialty products such as custom kitchen equipment for hotels and restaurants.

The best way to learn sheet metal work is through a four-year apprenticeship program. Apprentices generally start at 45 to 55 percent of the journeyman's pay rate.

Apprentice applicants can expect to take a math test before entry to the program and should have a background in math through trigonometry, plus classes in mechanical drawing, drafting, metal shop, and blueprint reading. Math is an important part of the classroom work for accepted apprentices.

Job opportunities for sheet metal workers are expected to be reasonably good through the 1980's.

STATIONARY ENGINEER

If you think of a stationary engineer as a power engineer, it is easier to understand what such a skilled person does. He operates and services the machinery that powers industry, lights cities, and controls the climate of large buildings. His primary responsibility is the safe operation and maintenance of all kinds of steam boilers, ranging from small units to huge steam plant boilers. Operating pressure in these boilers may range from less than 15 pounds to over 450 pounds per square inch. He also looks after other equipment such as heat exchangers, pumps, motors, turbines, generators, air compressors, air-conditioning units, and refrigeration equipment.

Stationary engineers typically work a forty-hour week that may include weekends and holidays. Often the power plant operates twenty-four hours a day, which means that the engineers work rotating shifts—day, swing, and graveyard.

Because power generation is becoming increasingly complicated, a four-year apprenticeship program is recommended. Apprentices start at 60 percent of the journeyman's rate, which in 1974 averaged $5.51 per hour. (Keep in mind that there are seldom layoffs in this trade.)

Algebra, geometry, physics, chemistry, and machine shop are suggested high-school classes for those interested in a future as a stationary engineer.

Opportunities for newly trained stationary engineers will remain rather steady through the 1980's, with 4,600 new apprentices needed each year nationwide.

Licensing requirements for stationary engineers vary from

state to state, making it difficult for an experienced worker to transfer to other locations.

Employers are hesitant to hire persons with diabetes, heart trouble, epilepsy, or other potentially disabling conditions, that might prove dangerous when working around such high-pressure equipment.

Some employers require workers to furnish their own hand tools.

Chapter **XXI**

Military Training as an Alternative

It is possible to serve four years in the military learning a trade and return to civilian life as a journeyman very much in demand as an employee.

The military, particularly the Navy and Air Force, offers training in a variety of highly skilled occupations. Their job titles—a plumber in the Navy is called a Utilitiesman (UT)—may differ somewhat from civilian titles, but the work done and the knowledge gained can be directly applicable to a civilian job.

Don't think of the military as an easy, sure route to a skill. It takes hard work, ambition, and study to become an electronic technician, electrician, steel worker, or heavy equipment operator either in or out of the service.

The first step is to visit the recruiters for each branch of the service. In general, you may enlist if you are between the ages of seventeen and thirty-one. High-school graduates are preferred. Talk with the recruiter about what jobs he has available and what guarantees you will have that you will be assigned in that particular career field. Women are eligible for training in some of the skilled trade fields.

Then, before you make any commitment, you take an aptitude test. The test is very much like a general IQ test and involves vocabulary and some simple math. A mechanical aptitude test may also be involved.

Your score determines which training you can select. Almost

everyone with at least average intelligence is able to pick a specific field for training.

Some jobs are related. If, for instance, your test scores do not qualify you to train as an auto mechanic, you may qualify to learn repair of the auto electrical systems.

As you talk with the recruiters and as you make career selections, keep in mind that there is very little demand in civilian life for parachute jumpers, infantrymen, or howitzer operators. There may be many good reasons for a person to become a parachute jumper, but if you are looking to the military for training in a salable skill, you should be choosing some other specialty for a career and doing your jumping on weekends.

Once you have made your decision and qualified through the aptitude test for specific training, you enlist. It is possible to enlist for only three years, but most recruiters agree that if you are trying to reach journeyman's level in a particular skill, you are more likely to get good learning assignments if you have signed up for four years. (In some selected occupations, the minimum enlistment is six years.)

For nine weeks you attend basic training, and then you begin your occupational training.

The military has some excellent schools. Depending on the skill, they may last from twelve to twenty-four weeks. In almost all occupations you should strive to attend one of these schools immediately after basic training. It will start you in the right learning direction.

If you are not selected for the training school, you will be learning your skills on the job or through correspondence courses on your own time. The harder you work in training schools, on the job, or by taking correspondence courses, the more interesting assignments you will get and the faster you will receive promotions. Promotions tend to happen more rapidly in skilled jobs than in the unskilled areas.

At any time during your military service you may be sent to

additional schools for training. It is not unusual, for instance, for an advanced Navy Construction Mechanic (heavy equipment mechanic in civilian life) to be sent to the Caterpillar factory for training on their earth-moving equipment. When a man is trained in this way, he finds civilian employment relatively easy to find, often with a Caterpillar distributor.

If you choose a training assignment and then find that you don't like the work, it will be difficult, but not impossible, to change career goals.

Says one Navy recruiter, "If you're not happy with the training, it is possible to flunk the tests so you don't get that particular rating. But then you're sent to the fleet unskilled and you're up for grabs by any section that needs a warm body. It's probably better to do the work you've been trained for well and work on your own for a 'cross rating.' "

"We had a boilerman who decided he wanted to be a hospital corpsman. When he was off duty, he hung around the hospital learning about the work and took all the correspondence courses on his own that he could. It didn't take long before the whole fleet, officers and men, were rooting for him. It took a while, but he got his transfer."

On the surface, military pay rates seem quite low. But because room, board, uniforms, full medical coverage, PX and commissary privileges are included, the effective rate of pay is competitive with many unskilled jobs. If you remember that you wouldn't be paid at all if you were just attending school, then some pay, however low, may be attractive.

In 1976 the entry pay for enlisted personnel was $361.20 per month. At the end of four years, given normal promotions, the pay rate should be $524.10 plus allowances for dependents.

It is, of course, possible to enter the service without selecting a particular career field. This may provide an opportunity for the young person to explore several career fields and then train on his own for some occupation that attracts him.

The list below is an example of the kinds of skill training available in the military, in this case the Navy. You should discuss current opportunities with your local recruiter.

Civilian Occupation	*Related Navy Occupation*	*Entry Requirements*
Aircraft electronics technician	Aviation Electronics Technician (AT)	Above-average intelligence, competence in arithmetic, electrical and mechanical aptitudes, normal vision and hearing.
Aircraft engine mechanic	Aviation Machinist's Mate (AD)	Good learning ability and mechanical aptitude.
Automotive mechanic	Aviation Support Equipment Technician (AS)	Good learning ability and aptitude for mechanical and electrical work.
Boiler operator	Boiler Technician (BT)	Good learning ability and mechanical aptitude.
Calibration equipment worker	Missile Technician (MT)	Good learning ability, normal hearing and color vision, and ability to pass submarine qualification test.
Construction electrician	Construction Electrician (CE)	Electrical and mechanical aptitude.
Construction equipment mechanic	Construction Mechanic (CM)	Good learning ability and mechanical aptitude.
Construction equipment operator	Equipment Operator (EO)	Physical strength, normal color vision, good learning ability, and mechanical aptitude.
Construction worker (carpenter, roofer, plasterer)	Builder (BU)	Good learning ability and high degree of mechanical aptitude.
Electrician	Electrician's Mate (EM)	Average learning ability, good aptitude for practical arithmetic and electrical work plus mechanical aptitude.
Electronics technician	Electronics Technician (ET)	Good learning ability and knowledge of arithmetic, mechanical aptitude, and interest in electronics; normal color vision.

Civilian Occupation	*Related Navy Occupation*	*Entry Requirements*
Engine lathe operator	Machinery Repairman (MR)	Mechanical aptitude and ability to work with figures.
Iron structural worker	Steelworker (SW)	Physical strength and ability to work in high places, mechanical aptitude, and knowledge of practical arithmetic.
Optical instrument repairman	Opticalman (OM)	Good learning ability, aptitude for close, exact work, and mechanical skill.
Plumber	Utilitiesman (UT)	Good learning ability and mechanical aptitude.
Printer	Lithographer (LI)	Good learning ability and near-vision, proficiency in spelling and grammar, ability to work with machinery and chemicals.
Surveyor	Engineering Aid (EA)	Above-average intelligence, background in algebra, geometry, and trigonometry, and aptitude for detail work.

If you are surprised by the variety of jobs available, even in a partial listing, remember that an aircraft carrier or an overseas military base is a city unto itself. Whenever civilian labor is not available, the military must provide all of the services and facilities necessary to operate independently.

Obviously, military service and training does not appeal to everyone. It will require you to move away from your familiar community. If you become a construction equipment operator, you may find yourself building a road in the antarctic or the Sahara, but you will be gaining experience that will be highly valued when you later apply for civilian jobs.

About six months before you expect to be discharged, you should start looking for employment. You may wish to make your initial inquiries by mail, including a brief résumé describing your military experience. Then you should take some of your leave time to visit prospective employers to convince them of your talents.

If you are interested in a union job such as carpenter, electrician, or plumber, you will have to take the local union's journeyman's test to qualify for that rating. You should make contact with the union to find out what kinds of questions will be asked. Keep in mind that electricians and plumbers must be able to pass a test on local building codes. You will have to study those on your own before you take the test.

Nonunion companies may also ask you to take a test so that they can evaluate your skill level.

And, of course, you may find the military to your liking and make that your career.